Collins | English for Exams

GET READY FOR IELTS: WRITING
PRE-INTERMEDIATE A2+

Fiona Aish & Jo Tomlinson

Collins

Published by Collins
An imprint of HarperCollins Publishers
1 Robroyston Gate,
Glasgow, G33 1JN

HarperCollins Publishers
Macken House
39/40 Mayor Street Upper
Dublin 1
D01 C9W8
Ireland

Second edition 2026

10 9 8 7 6 5 4 3 2 1

© HarperCollins Publishers 2012, 2026

ISBN 978–0–00–876545–3

Collins® is a registered trademark of HarperCollins Publishers Limited

collins.co.uk/elt

A catalogue record for this book is available from the British Library

Typeset by Davidson Pre-Press Ltd

Printed in the UK by Ashford Colour Ltd.

All rights reserved. No part of this book may be reproduced, stored in a retrieval system, or transmitted in any form or by any means, electronic, mechanical, photocopying, recording or otherwise, without the prior permission in writing of the Publisher. This book is sold subject to the conditions that it shall not, by way of trade or otherwise, be lent, re-sold, hired out or otherwise circulated without the Publisher's prior consent in any form of binding or cover other than that in which it is published and without a similar condition including this condition being imposed on the subsequent purchaser.

Without limiting the exclusive rights of any author, contributor or the publisher of this publication, any unauthorised use of this publication to train generative artificial intelligence (AI) technologies is expressly prohibited. HarperCollins also exercise their rights under Article 4(3) of the Digital Single Market Directive 2019/790 and expressly reserve this publication from the text and data mining exception.

HarperCollins does not warrant that collins.co.uk/elt or any other website mentioned in this title will be provided uninterrupted, that any website will be error free, that defects will be corrected, or that the website or the server that makes it available are free of viruses or bugs. For full terms and conditions please refer to the site terms provided on the website.

Entered words that we have reason to believe constitute trademarks have been designated as such. However, neither the presence nor absence of such designation should be regarded as affecting the legal status of any trademark.

If you would like to comment on any aspect of this book, please contact us at the given address or online.
E-mail: collins.elt@harpercollins.co.uk

Author: Fiona Aish, Jo Tomlinson
Project lead: James Maroney
Editor: Julie Moore
For the Publisher: Gillian Bowman, Fiona McGlade
Typesetter: Davidson Pre-Press Ltd, UK
Printer: Ashford Colour Ltd, UK

Acknowledgements

We would like to thank those authors and publishers who kindly gave permission for copyright material to be used in the Collins Corpus. We would also like to thank Times Newspapers Ltd for providing valuable data.

Photo credits

All images © Shutterstock.com

About the authors

Fiona Aish and **Jo Tomlinson** have been preparing students for exams for over 20 years and have written more than 15 books together. They are DELTA qualified and have an MA in Applied Linguistics and Language Testing respectively. They use their knowledge and experience to inform their teaching, teacher training, and materials development. They also work as item writers and test consultants. Find out more about them at: www.target-english.eu

Contents

Unit title		Topic	Exam focus	Page
Introduction				4
1	Hobbies and interests	Sports and activities	Analysing and describing a table for Task 1	10
2	Education	School, college and university	Analysing and describing a bar chart for Task 1	16
3	Culture	Music, art and television	Writing a Task 2 opinion essay	22
Review 1				28
4	Family	Relationships	Structuring a Task 2 opinion essay	30
5	Tourism	Holidays and travel	Analysing and describing a line graph for Task 1	36
6	Films	Genres and formats	Analysing and describing a pie chart for Task 1	42
Review 2				48
7	Technology	Computers, the internet and mobile phones	Describing advantages and disadvantages for a Task 2 essay	50
8	Happiness	Money and relationships	Writing about opinions for a Task 2 essay	56
9	The natural world	The environment and pollution	Describing a process for Task 1	62
Review 3				68
10	Places to live	People and places	Comparing and contrasting multiple charts and graphs for Task 1	70
11	Health	Healthcare and lifestyles	Writing a cause and effect essay for Task 2	76
12	Transport	Public and private transport	Writing a problem and solution essay for Task 2	82
Review 4				88
Practice test				90
Answer key				92
Glossary				116

Introduction

Who is this book for?

Get Ready for IELTS Writing has been written for learners with a band score of 3 or 4 who want to achieve a higher score. Using this book will help you improve your pre-intermediate speaking skills for the IELTS Academic Writing test.

You can use *Get Ready for IELTS Writing*:

- as a self-study course. We recommend that you work systematically through the 12 units in order to benefit from its progressive structure.
- as a supplementary writing skills course for IELTS preparation classes. The book provides enough material for approximately 50 hours of classroom activity.

Get Ready for IELTS Writing

- The book contains **12 units**. Each unit focuses on a different topic and these topics are ones that often appear in the IELTS exam.
- After every three units, there is a **Review unit** which helps you to revise the language and skills covered in the previous units.
- At the end of the book the **Practice test** gives you the opportunity to take an IELTS-style test under test conditions.
- There is also a full **answer key** at the back of the book so you can check your answers. Here you will find suggested answers for more open-ended questions and model answers for the exam practice questions in Part 3 of the unit.
- The **glossary** at the back of the book lists the useful words from each unit with their Cobuild dictionary definitions.

Unit structure

Each unit starts with the **Aims** of the unit. They outline the key language and skills covered.

Part 1: Language development provides exercises on vocabulary related to the topic as well as key grammar related to the IELTS Task covered in the unit. Clear structures are provided.

Part 2: Skills development focuses on either a Task 1 or a Task 2 question and provides step-bystep exercises and guidance on the type of essay answer required and the key stages of the writing process. The particular requirements of each type of essay question and the different formats for presenting information (tables, bar charts, line graphs, pie charts, etc.) are clearly explained..

Part 3: Exam practice provides one exam practice question for either Task 1 or Task 2 in a format that follows the actual exam. You can use this to check whether or not you are ready for the test.

Finally, a **Progress check** helps you to check whether you have covered the key points in the unit.

Other features

Exam information boxes in each unit provide key background information about the IELTS Writing exam.

Exam tip boxes provide essential exam techniques and strategies.

Watch out! boxes highlight common errors often made in the exam.

Study tips
- Each unit contains approximately three hours of study material.
- Try to answer the questions without looking at a dictionary to develop the skill of guessing the meaning of unknown words from context. This is important because dictionaries cannot be used during the actual exam.
- Use a pencil to complete the exercises, so that you can erase your first answers and do the exercises again for revision.
- Try to revise what you have learnt in Parts 1 and 2 before doing the practice IELTS questions in Part 3. This will improve the quality of your answers, and using the new language will help you to remember it.
- It's recommended that you try and complete all questions in the unit as the skills needed to do well at the IELTS test can only be improved through extensive practice.
- Read the answer key carefully as this provides information on what kind of answer is awarded high marks.
- Part 3 contains exam practice with timed questions. This gives you the opportunity to practise writing to a time limit. If you find this difficult at first, you could focus first on writing a high quality response of the correct length. Then you could start to reduce the time allowed gradually until you are able to write an acceptable answer within the time limit..
- You should become familiar enough with your own hand-writing so that you can accurately estimate the number of words you have written at a glance.

Other resources
Also available in the *Collins Get Ready for IELTS* series are: *Reading*, *Listening* and *Speaking*.

Free Teacher's Notes for all units are available online at: collins.co.uk/eltresources

The International English Language Testing System (IELTS) test

IELTS is jointly managed by the British Council, Cambridge ESOL Examinations and IDP Education, Australia. There are two versions of the test:
- Academic
- General Training

Academic is for students wishing to study at undergraduate or postgraduate levels in an English-medium environment.
General Training is for people who wish to migrate to an English-speaking country. This book is primarily for students taking the Academic version.

The test
There are four modules:

Listening 30 minutes, plus 10 minutes for transferring answers to the answer sheet.
NB: the audio is heard only once.
Approx. 10 questions per section
Section 1: two speakers discuss a social situation
Section 2: one speaker talks about a non-academic topic
Section 3: up to four speakers discuss an educational project
Section 4: one speaker gives a talk of general academic interest

Reading 60 minutes
3 texts, taken from authentic sources, on general, academic topics. They may contain diagrams, charts, etc.
40 questions: may include multiple choice, sentence completion, completing a diagram, graph or chart, choosing headings, yes/no, true/false questions, classification and matching exercises.

Writing Task 1: 20 minutes: description of a table, chart, graph or diagram (150 words minimum)
Task 2: 40 minutes: an essay in response to an argument or problem (250 words minimum)

Speaking 11–14 minutes
A three-part face-to-face oral interview with an examiner. The interview is recorded.
Part 1: introductions and general questions (4–5 mins)
Part 2: individual long turn (3–4 mins) – the candidate is given a task, has one minute to prepare, then talks for 1–2 minutes, with some questions from the examiner.
Part 3: two-way discussion (4–5 mins): the examiner asks further questions on the topic from Part 2, and gives the candidate the opportunity to discuss more abstract issues or ideas.

Timetabling Listening, Reading and Writing must be taken on the same day, and in the order listed above. Speaking can be taken up to 7 days before or after the other modules.

Scoring Each section is given a band score. The average of the four scores produces the Overall Band Score. You do not pass or fail IELTS; you receive a score.

IELTS and the Common European Framework of Reference

The CEFR shows the level of the learner and is used for many English as a Foreign Language examinations. The table below shows the approximate CEFR level and the equivalent IELTS Overall Band Score:

CEFR description	CEFR level	IELTS Band Score
Proficient user (Advanced)	C2	9
	C1	7–8
Independent user (Intermediate – Upper Intermediate)	B2	5–6.5
	B1	4–5

This table contains the general descriptors for the band scores 1–9:

IELTS Band Scores		
9	Expert user	Has fully operational command of the language: appropriate, accurate and fluent with complete understanding.
8	Very good user	Has fully operational command of the language, with only occasional unsystematic inaccuracies and inappropriacies. Misunderstandings may occur in unfamiliar situations. Handles complex detailed argumentation well.
7	Good user	Has operational command of the language, though with occasional inaccuracies, inappropriacies and misunderstandings in some situations. Generally handles complex language well and understands detailed reasoning.
6	Competent user	Has generally effective command of the language despite some inaccuracies, inappropriacies and misunderstandings. Can use and understand fairly complex language, particularly in familiar situations.
5	Modest user	Has partial command of the language, coping with overall meaning in most situations, though is likely to make many mistakes. Should be able to handle basic communication in own field.
4	Limited user	Basic competence is limited to familiar situations. Has frequent problems in understanding and expression. Is not able to use complex language.
3	Extremely limited user	Conveys and understands only general meaning in very familiar situations. Frequent breakdowns in communication occur.
2	Intermittent user	No real communication is possible except for the most basic information using isolated words or short formulae in familiar situations and to meet immediate needs. Has great difficulty understanding spoken and written English.
1	Non user	Essentially has no ability to use the language beyond possibly a few isolated words.
0	Did not attempt the test	No assessable information provided.

Marking

The Listening and Reading papers have 40 items, each worth one mark if correctly answered. Here are some examples of how marks are translated into band scores:

Listening:
16 out of 40 correct answers: band score 5
23 out of 40 correct answers: band score 6
30 out of 40 correct answers: band score 7

Reading:
15 out of 40 correct answers: band score 5
23 out of 40 correct answers: band score 6
30 out of 40 correct answers: band score 7

Writing and Speaking are marked according to performance descriptors.

Writing: examiners award a band score for each of four areas with equal weighting:
- Task achievement (Task 1)
- Task response (Task 2)
- Coherence and cohesion
- Lexical resource and grammatical range and accuracy

Speaking: examiners award a band score for each of four areas with equal weighting:
- Fluency and coherence
- Lexical resource
- Grammatical range
- Accuracy and pronunciation

For full details of how the examination is scored and marked, go to: www.ielts.org

The IELTS Test: Formats

There are two formats for the IELTS test. One is paper-based, and the other is computer-based. The difference is in the test-taking experience, not in the content. Both test formats have the same questions and marking criteria. The Speaking part of the test is conducted face to face with an examiner for both the paper and computer based tests.

The formats are different as follows:

Delivery

- **Paper-based** – The candidate writes their answers for the Listening, Reading, and Writing sections on physical paper using a pen or pencil.
- **Computer-based** – The candidate types their answers for the Listening, Reading, and Writing sections on a desktop computer.

Test Environment

- **Paper-based** – Tests are held in large rooms with many other candidates.
- **Computer-based** – Tests are conducted in smaller rooms with fewer candidates, and each candidate has their own computer station.

Listening Test

- **Paper-based** – Candidates listen to the audio recording played through speakers in the room. Candidates have 10 minutes at the end of the Listening test to transfer their answers from the question booklet to the answer sheet.
- **Computer-based** – Candidates wear headphones and listen individually. Candidates have 2 minutes at the end of the Listening test to review their answers because the answers are typed directly into the computer as candidates listen.

Reading Test

- **Paper-based** – Candidates read the passages and answer the questions in a physical booklet. Candidates can highlight or underline text with a pen or pencil.
- **Computer-based** – Candidates see the passages and questions side-by-side on a screen and type their answers into the computer. Candidates can use on-screen tools to highlight text and make notes.

Writing Test

- **Paper-based** – Candidates write their essays by hand. Candidates must write clearly. Candidates have to count their words manually.

- **Computer-based** – Candidates type their essays using a keyboard. Candidates can use cut, copy, and paste to edit their texts. The screen provides a live word count.

Results

- **Paper-based** – Results are typically available 13 calendar days after the test date.

- **Computer-based** – Results are available much faster, usually within 1 to 5 days.

Scoring

Each section is given a band score. The average of the four scores produces the Overall Band Score. You do not pass or fail IELTS; you receive a score.

1 Hobbies and interests

Language development | Hobbies and interests, The present simple, Quantifiers
Exam skills | Describing tables, Writing an introduction
Exam practice | Task 1

Part 1: Language development

Vocabulary: Hobbies and interests

1 Look at the pictures of hobbies, then fill each gap below with the correct verb + noun.

> **Gabrielle:** I have lots of hobbies. Every weekend I (1) ___*play golf*___ with my father. There is a club nearby, so we go there. It's really good fun, but it's much better being on the course if the weather is nice and sunny. My father is a better player than me. I usually take four or five shots to get the ball in the hole. In the evenings I (2) _____ a lot. I especially like dramas and reality shows.
>
> **Yuan:** I like sports quite a lot. I (3) _____ three times a week! There is a pool near my house, so I usually go there before school. I really love it! I also (4) _____ to _____ a lot. My favourite singers are Harry Styles and Taylor Swift. I use my headphones at home because my mother doesn't like the loud noise!

2 It is important to use the correct verbs with hobbies and interests. Put the hobbies under the correct verbs in the table. (Some hobbies may be used with more than one verb.)

swimming   shopping   football   gymnastics   karate   yoga   computer games
the violin   the guitar   skating   TV   horse riding   golf

do	go	play	watch
	swimming		

Writing for IELTS

Unit 1

Grammar: present simple

We use the present simple to describe repeated or regular activities.

I play (present simple) *football* (activity) *every week.*

We also use the present simple to talk about things we like / don't like / love / hate. These verbs can be followed by another verb in the -ing form.

I like (like verb) *going* (-ing form) *swimming.*

3 Complete the text using the present simple tense.

I asked the people in my class about their hobbies, and this is what I found out. The boys like (1) _playing_ karate, but not the girls. Ellen hates (2) _____ karate. Brian doesn't like (3) _____ swimming. He never (4) _____ swimming but Julia and Pamela (5) _____ swimming four times a week. John and Paul love (6) _____ football. They (7) _____ football every day. Ellen is the only girl that (8) _____ football.

	Boys					Girls		
	Arnold	Peter	John	Paul	Brian	Ellen	Julia	Pamela
Football	x4 a week		every day!	every day!		x2 a week		
Swimming	x2 a week	x3 a week	x2 a week		Never!		x4 a week	x4 a week
Karate	every day	every day	every day	x2 a week	x3 a week	Never!		

Grammar: Quantifiers

4 There are many different words to describe quantity. Put the words from the box in the correct order from 0 (the smallest amount) to 100 (the largest amount).

0 _____ _all_ 100

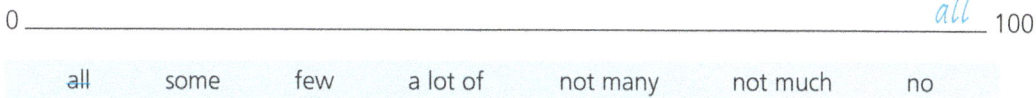

| all | some | few | a lot of | not many | not much | no |

Look at the information in the table in Exercise 3 and complete the sentences below with the correct quantity words.

1. ____A lot of____ boys like football.
2. _____ the students have at least one hobby.
3. _____ girls like karate.
4. _____ students go swimming.
5. _____ students play football every day.

Hobbies and interests

Part 2: Skills development

> **Exam information: Writing Task 1**
> In Task 1 of the writing paper, you need to describe some visual information, such as a table, chart or diagram. You need to describe the key points in the visual using formal or semi-formal writing. You have 20 minutes to do this task, and you must write 150 words or more.

> **Exam information: Describing tables**
> In Task 1, you might need to describe a table. A table has information in *rows* (going across) and *columns* (going down). The table will have a heading at the top to show the topic. There will usually be headings for the rows and columns to show the categories or groups.

1 Look at the table. Circle the correct option in each sentence below.

Class Sports Survey		
Sport	Number of students who like it	Number of students who don't like it
Tennis	8	2
Football	5	5
Hockey	3	7
Cricket	0	10

1 Football / **Tennis** is the most popular sport in the class.
2 A lot of students don't like *football / hockey*.
3 *Football / Hockey* is liked and disliked by the same number of students.
4 Few students dislike *tennis / football*.
5 All the students dislike *cricket / football*.

2 Now look at this table and write T (True) or F (False) next to each sentence. Give reasons for your answers.

Number of hours a week spent on activities by age range					
Age range	Football	Swimming	Television	Computer games	Music
13–15 years	5	2	6	7	3
16–18 years	4	1.5	9	14	12

Writing for IELTS

1   Older teenagers spend a lot of time swimming. *F*
2   All older teenagers like playing computer games.
3   Listening to music is more popular with older teenagers.
4   Teenagers don't spend much time swimming.
5   Younger teenagers spend a lot of hours listening to music.

Exam tip: Identifying key points

In the table, make sure you understand:
(a) the main heading / title of the table
(b) the column headings / categories and exactly what these show.

Look for the most important information in the table by comparing categories and groups. Notice any similarities, any differences, any obvious changes and / or trends. These are what you will need to write about in your answer.

3   Look at the table below, then choose the sentence, a, b or c, which best explains what the table shows.

% of time spent on online activity, by age group					
Age group	Shopping	Social media	Reading news	Watching videos	Playing games
10–15 years	0	23	2	5	70
16–20 years	10	51	8	10	21
21–29 years	24	44	8	6	16
30–39 years	35	25	16	14	10
40–49 years	29	10	30	19	2
50+ years	10	5	54	23	1

a   The table shows how much time people spend online.
b   The table shows how much time people spend on online activities depending on their age.
c   The table shows the percentage of time spent on online activities by age group.

Exam tip: Writing an introduction

Use the following structure for the introduction to a Task 1 answer:
- One sentence to explain what the table shows. (Use different words from the words used in the heading for the table wherever possible.)
- One or two sentences summarizing the information shown in the table.
- Do not include details in the introduction. Save the details for the main part of your text, after the introduction.

4 Read two different introductions (A and B) to a text about the table in Exercise 3 and answer the questions.

1. Circle all the verbs in the introductions. What tense are the verbs?
2. Look at the first sentence of each introduction. Do these sentences accurately explain the title of the table?
3. Underline any details in A and B.
4. Which introduction is better, A or B? Why?

Introduction A: The table shows how much time the age groups spend on different types of online activity. There are six age ranges in the table from 10–15 to over 50. The online activities include shopping, social media and playing games.

Introduction B: The table shows how much people like the internet depending on their age. 70% of children between ages 10–15 play games online, and no children between ages 10–15 like shopping. Most older people read news sites. They spend 54% of their time reading the news online.

5 Now complete the rest of the text about the table, using the words from the box.

In general there are many differences depending on age group. The table shows that (1) _____ spend a lot of time playing games, but older people do not spend (2) _____ time playing games. Younger people spend more time on social media than older people, especially the age range (3) _____ . They spend 51% of their time on social media. Most age groups shop online except for the age group (4) _____ . (5) _____ people in this age group shop online. Reading news and watching videos is popular with (6) _____ age groups. Overall, young people like playing games and social media but older people (7) _____ reading news and (8) _____ on the internet.

16–20	younger age groups		10–15		
shopping	older	like	much	No	

Exam tip: Using the right tense

Always use the present tense to describe a table, unless it contains information about a time in the past or if past dates, e.g. years, are used as categories.

14 Writing for IELTS

Part 3: Exam practice

Writing Task 1

You should spend about 20 minutes on this task.

The table below shows the television viewing figures for sports by country, in millions.

Summarize the information by selecting and reporting the main features, and make comparisons where relevant.

Write at least 100 words.

Television viewing figures for sports by country, in millions					
Country	Tennis	Golf	Motor racing	Athletics	Totals
Australia	6.2	4.5	3.7	3	17.4
UK	6.6	2.8	6.4	4.5	20.3
USA	7	11.2	1.5	5.5	25.2
Canada	6.1	3.4	1.1	3.9	14.5
Total	25.9	21.9	12.7	16.9	

⮕ Progress Check

How many boxes can you tick? You should work towards being able to tick them all.

Did you...
make sure you understood the title, headings and categories of the table? ☐
use the present simple to describe the table (if the information in the table is about the present)? ☐
use quantifiers accurately to describe quantities? ☐
use the introduction to describe the table in general? ☐

2 Education

Language development | Education vocabulary, The past simple, Comparisons
Exam skills | Describing a bar chart, Beginning a paragraph
Exam practice | Task 1

Part 1: Language development

Vocabulary: Education

1 Look at the pictures. Complete the sentences by putting the letters of the bold words in the correct order.

1 At school, you have **s a l c s e s** _classes_ for different subjects, such as maths, science and history.
2 The **e t r e a h c** _____ will answer any questions you may have.
3 Sometimes at the end of the year, students take an **m e a x** _____ to check what they have learnt.
4 Some students go on to university, where they will learn through seminars and **c t u r s e l e** _____ .
5 Sometimes a university student gives a **s e i n r t a p n e t o** _____ to other students.

2 When you learn new vocabulary, try to learn which words usually go together (or collocate). Put the verbs in the box next to the nouns in the table. (You can use each verb more than once, and each noun can have more than one verb.)

take   sit   do   give   write   study   make   pass   fail   get

verbs	nouns	verbs	nouns
take	an exam		an essay
	a qualification		a subject (e.g. biology)
	a course		a presentation

16 Writing for IELTS

3 Complete the text with verbs from the table.

Mustafa: I have just finished school. I (1) _passed_ all my exams so I am really happy! I'm going to go to university. I want to (2) _____ Engineering. I have to (3) _____ an entrance exam for my English because I want to study in Australia. The course sounds really good. It's at a really good university and has a mixture of assessments; I'll need to (4) _____ essays, (5) _____ presentations and (6) _____ exams. I will also get some work experience! It's a lot of work but I think I will (7) _____ a really good qualification.

> **Watch out**
> To pass an exam means to reach the required grade or pass mark, not to take the exam.

Grammar: Past simple

4 The notes show what the class of 2023 did after they left school. Because the information refers to a time in the past, we must use past tense verbs to describe it. Complete the sentences below with the correct past tense forms of the verbs in brackets and the correct numbers from the notes:

Destinations of school leavers, 2023
University:	12 boys	14 girls
Local college:	7 boys	1 girl
Work:	5 boys	8 girls

1 _Fourteen_ girls _went_ (go) to university after leaving school.
2 _____ girl _____ (start) college.
3 _____ boys and _____ girls _____ (start) work straight after school.
4 _____ school leavers _____ (continue) studying after leaving school.
5 Only _____ school leavers _____ (not go) to university or college.
6 _____ school leavers _____ (decide) to go to college.

Grammar: Comparisons

We can also use comparative forms to compare items. Look at the information below:

> Student numbers at local primary schools, 2021
> Percival School: 80 boys   40 girls
> St James School: 100 boys   100 girls
> Roysters School: 60 boys   80 girls
> Bilsing School: 35 boys   35 girls

As much / many + noun + *as* (to show a quantity is the same):
St James School had as many boys as girls in 2021.

Not as much / many + noun + *as* + noun (to show that a quantity is less):
Percival School didn't have as many girls as St James School.

More + noun + *than* + noun (to show one quantity is larger than another):
Percival School had more boys than girls.

Less / fewer + noun + *than* + noun (to show one quantity is smaller than another):
Percival School had fewer boys than St James School.

5 Complete the sentences about Roysters and Bilsing schools using the words in brackets and the expressions above.

1. Roysters School had ____*more girls than boys*____ (girls / boys) in 2021.
2. Bilsing School had _____ (boys / girls).
3. Roysters School had _____ (boys / girls)
4. Bilsing School had _____ (students) Roysters School.
5. Roysters School had _____ (students) Bilsing School.

 **Watch out**

'Fewer' is used for countable nouns and 'less' for uncountable nouns.

Part 2: Skills development

Exam information: Describing a bar chart

For Task 1 of the writing paper you may need to describe a bar chart. Bar charts are useful for comparing the quantities of different categories (shown in the form of bars). Bar charts usually show the numbers or percentages on the left-hand vertical axis and the different categories that are being measured along the horizontal or bottom axis (plural: axes). Both axes are labelled to show what they refer to. Sometimes each category along the horizontal axis can be divided into two further sub-groups, e.g. boys / girls, so that these different sub-groups can be compared.

1 The bar chart below shows the information about student numbers at primary schools from Exercise 4 in Part 1. Answer the questions about the bar chart.

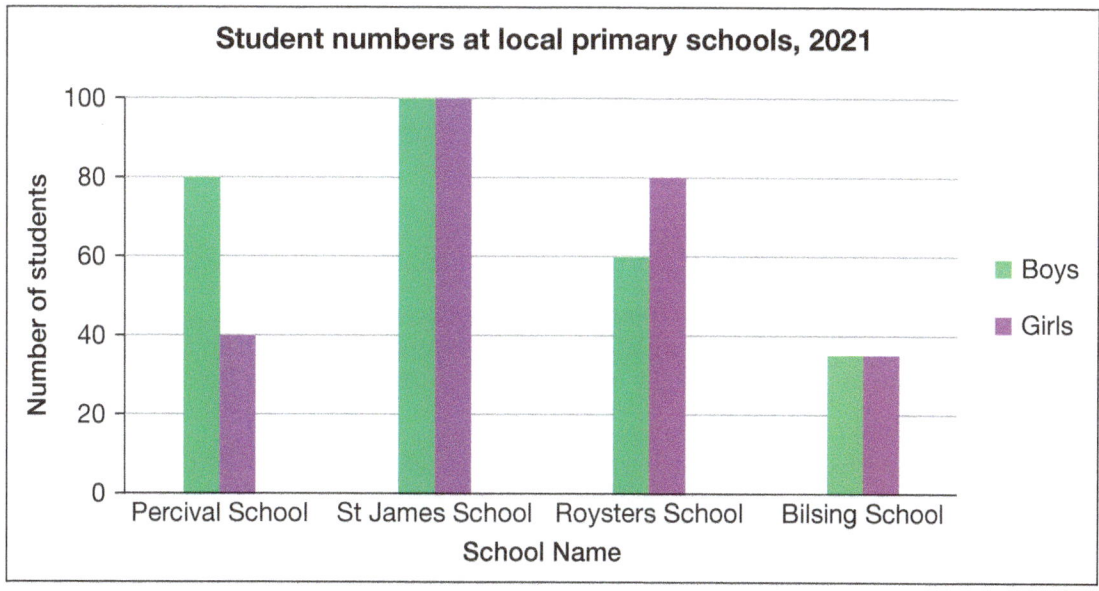

1 What do the numbers on the vertical axis measure?
2 How is the information grouped on the horizontal axis?
3 What do the different shades of the bars show?
4 When was the data collected?

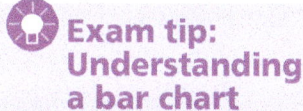 **Exam tip: Understanding a bar chart**

When you first see a bar chart, ask yourself the questions in Exercise 1 and the answers will give you the essential information for understanding it. Make sure you know which units are being used to measure quantities.

2 Look at the following bar chart. Read the introduction to a text about it, then complete the paragraph about the girls using the phrases from the box.

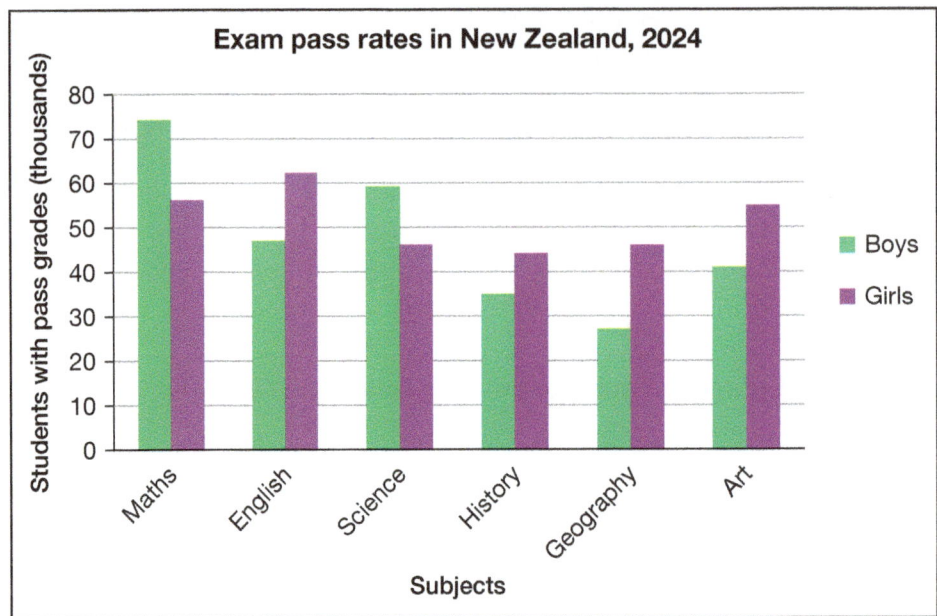

This bar chart shows the numbers (in thousands) of students with pass grades in different subject exams in Wales in 2003. The chart groups the students according to subject and divides these subject groups into boys and girls. There are clear differences between the boys and the girls.

Similar numbers of girls achieved pass grades in all the subjects. The number of girls with pass grades ranged from the highest number of just over (1) ___60 thousand___ to the lowest number of just over (2) _____, a difference of around (3) _____ Girls did best in Art, Maths and (4) _____, while their lowest pass rate was in (5) _____ Girls achieved (6) _____ passes than boys in four subjects: English (7) _____, History and (8) _____ .

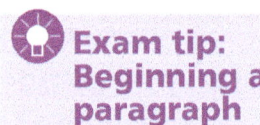

60 thousand		more
40 thousand	English	Geography
20 thousand	History	Art

Exam tip: Beginning a paragraph

Begin a main text paragraph with a sentence summarizing the information in general (e.g. *Similar numbers of girls gained pass grades in all the subjects.*), and follow this with sentences giving specific details.

3 Write a paragraph describing the boys' results shown in the bar chart in Exercise 2. Begin with a general sentence about the boys' pass rates, then give specific details and numbers. Use the paragraph about the girls as a model; the words and phrases in the box will also help you. Write approximately 90 words.

| however | range from (number) to (number) | just over / just under |
| | difference | highest / lowest | pass rate | achieve |

Writing for IELTS

Part 3: Exam practice

Writing Task 1

You should spend about 20 minutes on this task.

The bar chart below shows the number of students who chose certain university subjects in 2023. Summarize the information by selecting and reporting the main features, and make comparisons where relevant.

Write at least 100 words.

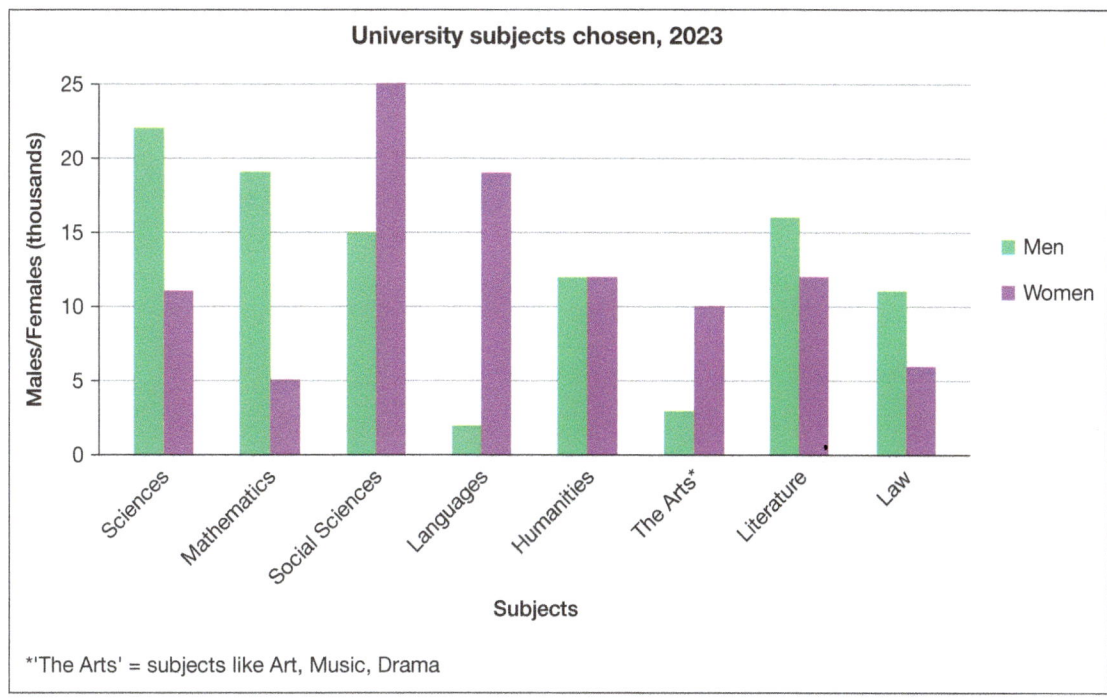

> ### Progress Check
>
> **How many boxes can you tick? You should work towards being able to tick them all.**
>
> Did you ...
> use common collocations (words that go together) correctly? ☐
> use comparison phrases to compare information? ☐
> make sure you understood which information the different axes of the bar chart show? ☐
> check the time period(s) shown in the bar chart? ☐
> write about the bar chart in general first, then add specific details afterwards? ☐

3 Culture

Language development | Cultural buildings, Adjectives, Word order, Conjunctions
Exam skills | Understanding essay questions
Exam practice | Task 2 Essay

Part 1: Language development

Vocabulary: Cultural buildings

a
_____

b
A museum

c
_____

d
_____

1 Label the pictures with the words from the box, then complete definitions 1–4.

architecture	an art gallery	a museum	a concert

1 __A museum__ contains objects from history.
2 _____ is a musical performance.
3 _____ means the design and creation of buildings.
4 _____ has collections of paintings and sculptures.

Vocabulary: Adjectives

Adjectives are used to describe things, experiences and people. Some adjectives are positive and some are negative.

The exhibition at the gallery was _boring_. (= negative)

Adele is a _fantastic_ *singer.* (= positive)

2 Decide if the adjectives in the box are positive (P) or negative (N). Write P or N next to each one.

| useful | dangerous _N_ | interesting | tiring | creative |
| amazing | beautiful | harmless | terrible | |

Unit 3

3 Now complete the texts below with adjectives from the box. (More than one answer may be possible.)

A: We went to the opera last weekend and I enjoyed it very much. The singers were (1) _amazing_ and the costumes were (2) _____ – all decorated with gold and jewels. The only bad part was that the performance was very long, three hours in total, so it was (3) _____ . I fell asleep as soon as we arrived home!

B: I definitely recommend the dinosaur exhibition at the Natural History Museum. It is really (1) _____ because it explains everything clearly. The exhibition is divided into two sections; one is about the (2) _____ dinosaurs that ate other dinosaurs and the other section is about the (3) _____ dinosaurs that just ate plants. The only bad thing about the exhibition is that some of the dinosaur drawings are (4) _____. They don't look like dinosaurs at all!

Grammar: Word order

The word order of a simple statement in English is: Subject + Verb + Object. Extra information usually comes after this structure.

Subject + Verb + Object + extra information
Picasso painted the picture at his studio in Paris.

4 Now put the words and phrases in sentences 1–6 in the correct order.

1 a film / on Saturday night / My family / watched
   My family watched a film on Saturday night.

2 a bestselling book / Louise / gave me / for my birthday
   _____

3 saw / a Shakespeare play / My sister and I / in London
   _____

4 has / many interesting art galleries / Tokyo / nowadays
   _____

5 opera / like / Older people / more than young people
   _____

6 online / music / Most teenagers / listen to
   _____

⚠ Watch out

English word order is not usually flexible. Don't change the order S + V + O.
The film I like very much. ✗   I like the film very much. ✓
I visited with my friend the art gallery. ✗   I visited the art gallery with my friend. ✓

Culture

Grammar: Word order

Conjunctions are words which connect short sentences together to make one longer sentence. The most common conjunctions are: and, but, because, so.

I watched a film on television yesterday. I went to the cinema yesterday. (two similar ideas)
I watched a film on television, *and* I went to the cinema yesterday.

I went to the rock concert. My friend recommended the rock concert. (action + reason)
I went to the rock concert, *because* my friend recommended it.

I like novels about history. I don't like novels about crime. (two different ideas)
I like novels about history, *but* I don't like novels about crime.

I enjoy taking photos. I bought a new camera. (reason + result)
I enjoy taking photos, *so* I bought a new camera.

5 Join the sentences using the conjunctions in brackets.

1 Maria likes reading detective novels. She likes reading books about history. (and)
___
___

2 My parents go to the cinema at weekends. They do not watch television at weekends. (but)
___
___

3 Young people should watch less television. Most programmes are not educational. (because)
___
___

4 The Science Museum is free. I think it is good for families. (so)
___
___

Part 2: Skills development

ℹ️ Exam information: A Task 2 essay
Task 2 in the IELTS exam asks a question about a social topic such as the environment, education or the media. You must write at least 250 words and you should spend about 40 minutes writing the essay.

ℹ️ Exam information: An Opinion Essay
Some essays will ask *How far do you agree with this statement?* Or *To what extent do you agree with this statement?* You must answer this question by giving your opinion as well as reasons and examples.

1 Read the following essay title.

> *All museums and art galleries should be free because they are an important part of a country's culture. How far do you agree with this statement?*

Which of the following is the topic of the essay, a, b or c?

a A country's culture
b The importance of museums and art galleries
c Free entrance to museums and art galleries

Which of the following questions has the same meaning as the essay question above?

1 How much do you agree that museums and art galleries are an important part of a country's culture?
2 How much do you agree that it is a good idea for museums and art galleries to be free for cultural reasons?
3 How much do you agree that museums and art galleries are good?

2 Read this essay question and tick the correct summary: a, b or c.

> *Children watch too much television nowadays and this is bad for their education and development. How far do you agree with this statement?*

a How much do you agree that if children watch too much television they do not learn or develop well?
b How much do you agree that television is bad for children?
c How much do you agree that watching television means that children learn nothing?

3 Do these ideas agree or disagree with the statement in the essay question in exercise 2? Write A (agree) or D (disagree) next to the ideas.

1 There are many interesting and educational programmes on television. ___
2 Watching too much television makes children lazy because they do less sport. ___
3 Watching some television is fine but watching too much television is bad for children. ___
4 Many children learn through visual activities, so watching television can help them. ___

> **Exam tip: Answer the question**
> Make sure you answer the question about the essay topic. Don't just write about the essay topic in general.

Which of these ideas do you agree with?

4 Read the essay question and decide if ideas 1–6 answer the question or just describe the topic in general. Write Q (question) or T (topic) next to each idea.

All children should learn to play a musical instrument at school. How far do you agree with this statement?

1 Music is fun for children so they enjoy it. *T*
2 Learning to play a musical instrument is a good idea because it helps children learn useful skills like coordination and self-motivation. ___
3 Learning to play a musical instrument is difficult so not all children can do it. ___
4 Listening to music helps children relax so it is good for their health. ___
5 Schools should include subjects such as music in the timetable because they are creative. ___
6 Learning a musical instrument at school is good but playing sport and other activities are also important for children. ___

5 Read the essay question below and complete the sentences with your own ideas.

Countries should not replace their traditional culture with modern culture. To what extent do you agree with this statement?

1 Traditional culture is important because *it helps people connect with the history of their country.*
2 Modern culture is important because _____
3 Young people often prefer modern culture but _____
4 Both traditional and modern culture are popular so _____

Now write four or five of your own ideas about the same essay topic. Give your reasons and use the conjunctions: and, but, because and so.

Part 3: Exam practice

Writing Task 2

You should spend about 40 minutes on this task.

Write about the following topic:

> Young people should spend more time on cultural activities such as music and theatre and less time on sport. How far do you agree with this statement?

Give reasons for your answer and include any relevant examples from your own knowledge or experience.

Write at least 175 words.

Exam tip: Think about ideas

In the IELTS test, spend two or three minutes thinking about your ideas before you start writing. Write your ideas down to help you remember them:

- You can make notes on the test paper
- You can make notes in the Notes section on screen

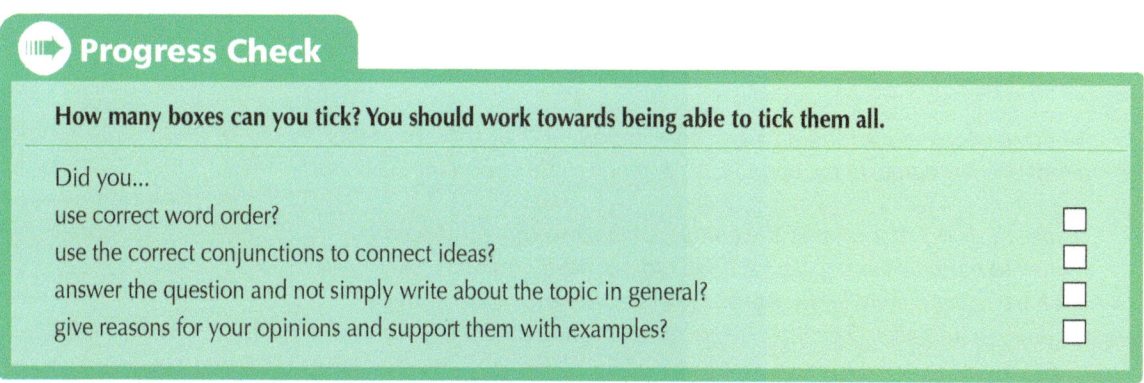

Review 1

1 Circle the correct option.

1 She likes watching television *but / and* she doesn't like playing computer games.
2 In 2024 the school *improved / improve* its computer facilities.
3 Most children *do / does* their homework in the evening.
4 I enjoy history lessons *so / because* I have a good teacher.
5 My father doesn't *playing / play* golf.
6 *Many / Much* museums are interesting for children nowadays.
7 My school has as *much / many* boys as girls.
8 I don't have as much homework *than / as* Jack.

2 Find seven more mistakes in this short essay and correct them.

> **The government should give more money to museums and art galleries and less money to sport.** How far do you agree with this statement?
>
> ~~All~~ Some people think museums are more important than sport but other people do not agree. In my opinion, art is much more important than sport.
>
> Firstly, art shows of a country the culture so the government should give money to museums and galleries. If we did not have museums, we would not have many culture in the world. However, it is expensive to run a museum or art gallery because the government should help pay for this.
>
> Sport is important too because it is fun and boring but people do not need many money to enjoy it. People playing sport in the park or they like watch it on television. These activities are cheap and they do not need money from the government.

3 Put the sentences describing the bar chart in the correct order by numbering them 1–5.

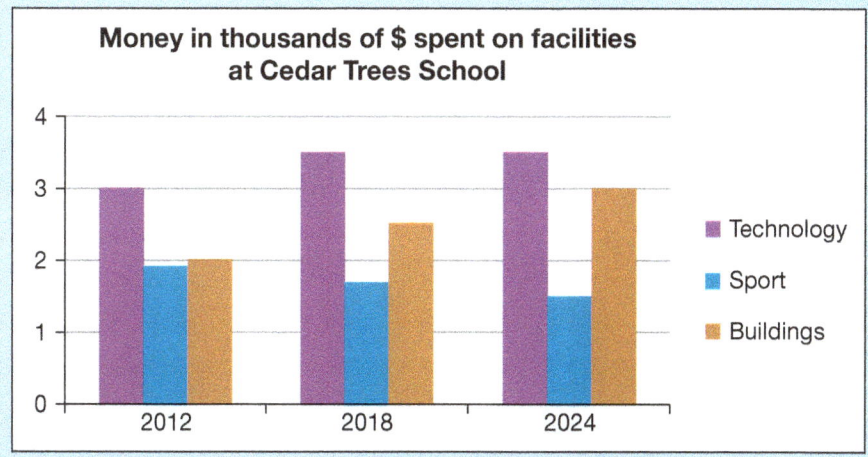

☐ From 2012 to 2024 the school increased the money spent on technology from $3,000 to $3,500.
☐ We can see that in general the school spent most money on technology.
☐ The graph shows how much money Cedar Trees School spent on different facilities from 2012 to 2024.
☐ However, not as much money was spent on sport in 2024; the money for sport went down from $2,000 to about $1,500.
☐ Also, the money for buildings rose from $2,000 to $3,000.

4 Decide if ideas 1–5 agree or disagree with this essay question. Write A (agree) or D (disagree) next to each idea.

> *Computer games are a part of modern culture like art and cinema. To what extent do you agree with this statement?*

1 Computer games are different from art but they are part of modern culture. ___
2 Art and cinema represent the culture of a country but computer games do not because they are not real. ___
3 Computer games are just entertainment so they are not part of modern culture. ___
4 Computer games often have excellent music and graphics so they are forms of art. ___
5 Computer games cannot be a part of modern culture because they are games. ___

4 Family

Language development | Family vocabulary, Modal verbs, Modal verbs for future opinions
Exam skills | Structuring a Task 2 essay, Paragraphs
Exam practice | Task 2 essay

Part 1: Language development

Vocabulary: Family members

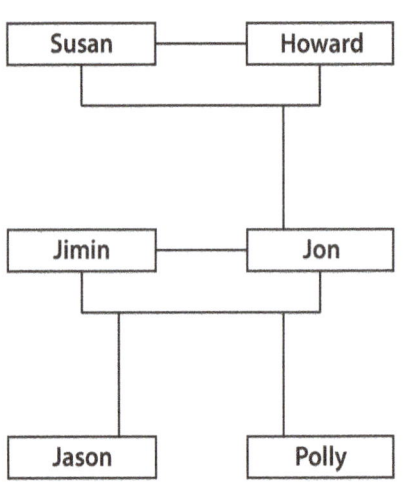

1 Complete the sentences about the family tree by putting the letters of the bold words in the correct order.

1 Jon's **o e r m h t** _mother_ is Susan.
2 Jon and Jimin's **o n s** _____ is Jason
3 Jon and Jimin's **u g r e d a h t** _____ is Polly.
4 Polly and Jason's **t e r f h a** _____ is Jon.
5 Polly and Jason's **e r r a m g o t n d h** _____ is Susan.
6 Jimin's **o m e t r h – n i – a w l** _____ is Susan.
7 Howard and Susan's **n g n o s a r d** _____ is Jason.
8 Jason and Polly's **r n s p e a t** _____ are Jimin and Jon.

Writing for IELTS

Unit 4

Grammar: Modal and semi-modal verbs

2   Read the speech bubbles, then complete the sentences below with the words in bold.

My name is Clare and I'm 15 years old. I go to school and this year I **will** have my first exams. I want to be a doctor, but it's a difficult job, so I **must** study hard to pass my exams. To be a doctor, I **must** have a lot of qualifications, but I **don't need to** be very good at art or languages, just science.

I'm Clare's mother, Molly. Clare wants to be a doctor when she is older. I think she **needs to** study hard for this. She plays on her computer quite a lot, which she **shouldn't** do. I think she **should** study more. She is clever. I think she **might** be a doctor.

1   ____will____ – used to talk about something expected in the future
2   _____ / have to / need to – used to say what is necessary
3   _____ – used to say something is a good idea
4   _____ – used to say something isn't a good idea
5   _____ – used to say it isn't necessary to do something
6   _____ / can / could – used to say what is possible
7   ____mustn't____ – used to say what isn't necessary

3   Rewrite the following sentences using the correct modal and semi-modal verbs from sentences 1–7 in Exercise 2.

1   It is a good idea for children to respect their parents.
    Children should respect their parents.
2   I plan to go to university in the future.
3   It is not a good idea for children to eat fast food.
4   It is possible that computers will do most jobs in the future.
5   It is necessary for all children to be taught basic skills like maths and reading.

Grammar: Modal verbs for future opinions

Use modal and semi-modal verbs to give your opinions about events in the future. Should / shouldn't, can, might and could are less definite than will, need to, must and have to. Compare:

Children who disobey their parents will be punished. (= a definite future action)
Children who disobey their parents should be punished. (= a suggestion)
Children who disobey their parents might be punished. (= a possibility)

4   Rewrite these sentences to make them less definite.

1   Children who don't study will fail their exams. (➔ a possibility)
2   University must prepare people for the best jobs. (➔ a suggestion)
3   Children need to follow their parents' advice. (➔ a suggestion)

Family

Part 2: Skills development

1 Look at the structure of a good example paragraph.

> I believe ¹the family is one of the most important structures in society. It is ²within the family that children can learn how to get on with other people and how to behave, and these things are important for life in the wider world. The family should also be a stable unit that ³provides love and support to children. Without this love and support, children might find it difficult to manage in the wider world. For example, children without loving, supportive parents could feel unable to do the things they would like to do, like go to university.

1. Main idea: *the family is important.*
2. Supporting idea which explains / adds to main idea: people *learn how to get on with others and how to behave in a family*
3. Supporting idea: *the family gives love and support.*

   Circled words = use of cautious language

Read these statements and write T (true) or F (false).

1 A paragraph should have more than one *main idea*. _____
2 A paragraph should have more than one *supporting idea*. _____
3 The first sentence of a paragraph should contain the *main idea* of the paragraph. _____
4 The last sentence of a paragraph should contain the *main idea* of the paragraph. _____
5 You should mainly use definite modal verbs, e.g. *will / must*. _____
6 You should mainly use less definite modal verbs, e.g. *can / might / could / should*. _____

2 Now read the following paragraphs and decide which one follows the rules in Exercise 1. What is wrong with the other two?

> **Paragraph A:** Children should learn rules from their parents. Teachers alone cannot teach a child rules. If a child doesn't have a strict home life, they could ignore the rules of the school and behave badly. Parents should teach a child rules from an early age so that when they reach school age they are more likely to behave and make friends with the other children at school.
>
> **Paragraph B:** Children will be really terrible if they have terrible parents. For example, some children in my school misbehave and their parents don't care. Although the teacher complains to the parents, the parents don't do anything about it. It is better for children if their parents teach them rules from an early age. Then the child will behave better. Rules must be taught by parents and teachers.
>
> **Paragraph C:** Rules are important things which must be taught by parents and teachers. Rules need to be taught by parents first because this will help when the child gets into school. If a child has no rules, he will misbehave. Also, beliefs need to be taught by parents. A child needs to learn their belief in things like religion from their parents. Parents should also teach a child some social skills, but a teacher should teach them school subjects.

Unit 4

ℹ️ Exam information: Paragraphs

An essay should be made up of separate paragraphs and the points within each paragraph should follow a logical order: firstly a main idea, followed by supporting ideas which explain or add to the main idea.

3 The first line of each paragraph below is missing. Write a first line which summarizes the main idea of the paragraph. The first one is done for you.

1 _Family structures are changing in the West._ Once, the traditional structure of two parents with two children was the most common family type in Western countries like the UK and the USA, but this is changing. New family structures include one-parent families and families with children from more than one marriage. These new family types are becoming increasingly common. Different family structures mean that many children live with a variety of full, step or half brothers and sisters.

2 _____ If children don't spend time with their parents, this could affect them because they are not receiving the attention they need to learn and develop. Many people claim that children are happy on their devices, but this doesn't give them social skills that they can learn doing activities with their parents.

3 _____ Having brothers and sisters means that a child learns how to socialize with other children from a young age and this is incredibly beneficial for them. They also grow up and grow old with an existing support network around them, which people with no brothers and sisters may not have. An only child can also be very lonely.

4 _____ It is not a child's job to cook, clean or help in the home. Children should be playing and having fun because childhood is the only time when they will be free from work. Children should be developing rather than becoming tired doing housework. Although many argue that helping in the home teaches children to look after their environment and to be clean, children can learn these things in other ways than through housework.

ℹ️ Exam information: Structuring an essay

Structuring an essay is an important part of writing for IELTS. For a Task 2 essay, use a standard essay structure consisting of separate paragraphs: an introduction (one paragraph), followed by the main body of the essay (two or three paragraphs), then a conclusion (one paragraph).

4 Put the paragraphs of this essay in the correct order by matching them to the headings below.

When children become teenagers, they should start to help their parents with tasks such as cooking, cleaning and shopping. How far do you agree with this statement?

A Helping with tasks around the home gives teenagers new skills and helps busy parents. For these reasons, I believe that teenagers should help with tasks such as cooking, cleaning, and shopping. This will also create a happier environment for everyone in the home.

B Also, sharing the household tasks often helps parents. Many parents work long hours outside the home and doing jobs at home after work can be very tiring. When teenagers do jobs around the house, it can help parents a lot and lower their stress. It might also teach teenagers about how much work their parents usually do at home. It might teach them to work as a team within their family too.

C There are lots of tasks to do around the home and normally the parents have to do them. Some people say that teenagers should help with these tasks. However, some people say that this is not necessary and teenagers should relax or study instead. In my opinion, I believe that teenagers should help around the house and that this is good for everyone in the family.

D Helping with household chores teaches teenagers lots of different valuable life skills. For example, learning to cook means they can prepare their own meals in the future. Cleaning their rooms helps them to understand how to keep a living space tidy and organised. Some people argue young people will learn these skills when they move out, but they are essential skills and it is easier to learn them when they are living at home.

Paragraph 1 (Introduction): _____

Paragraph 2: _____

Paragraph 3: _____

Paragraph 4 (Conclusion): _____

5 Now match the parts of an essay to their different functions.

1 Introduction _____
2 Main body _____
3 Conclusion _____

a Gives some general information about the essay topic, may put forward some differing opinions and gives an answer to the essay question.

b Summarizes all the arguments and restates your answer / opinion.

c Describes and explains different viewpoints, arguments, advantages and disadvantages, supported by examples.

> **Exam tip: Introductions**
>
> The introduction to a Task 2 essay can describe the topic of the essay, give background information to it and list various opinions about it. You should also briefly state your own view, which you then go on to explain and support in the main body of the essay.

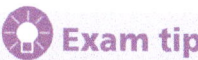

Part 3: Exam practice

Writing Task 2

You should spend about 40 minutes on this task.

Write about the following topic:

Children should always follow their parents' advice.
To what extent do you agree or disagree with this statement?

Give reasons for your answer and include any relevant examples from your own knowledge or experience.

Write at least 175 words.

Exam tip

The instruction says you can include any relevant examples from you own knowledge or experience. You can introduce this information with phrases like: *for example, for instance, in my own family/country/culture/ experience.*

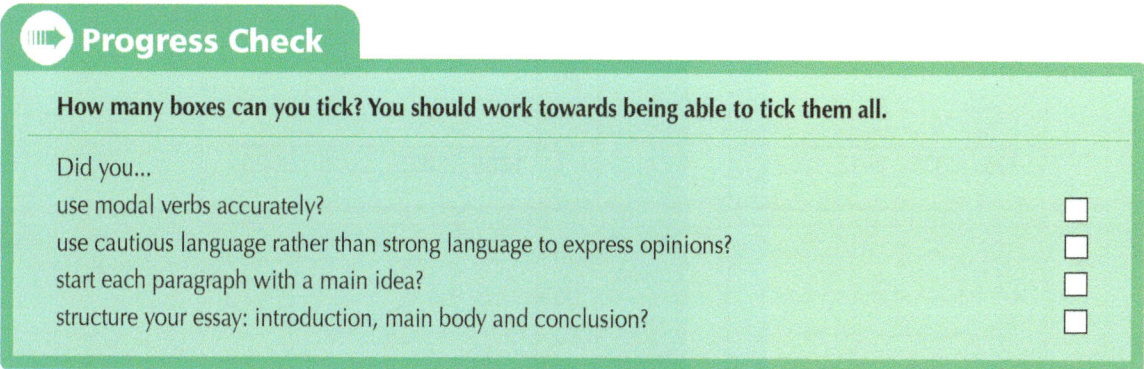

Progress Check

How many boxes can you tick? You should work towards being able to tick them all.

Did you...
use modal verbs accurately? ☐
use cautious language rather than strong language to express opinions? ☐
start each paragraph with a main idea? ☐
structure your essay: introduction, main body and conclusion? ☐

5 Tourism

Language development | Language for describing trends, Expressions with time
Exam skills | Describing line graphs, Tenses in Task 1
Exam practice | Task 1

Part 1: Language development

Vocabulary: Verbs and nouns to describe trends

You can use certain verbs to describe changes in the lines on line graphs.

1. Match the verbs in the box to the lines on these line graphs. Write either 1, 2, 3 or 4 next to each verb.

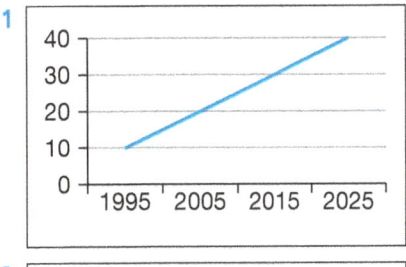
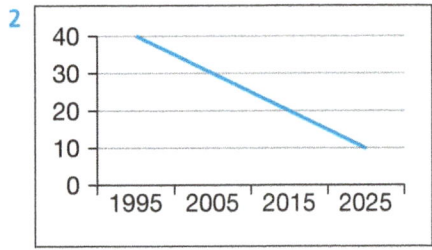
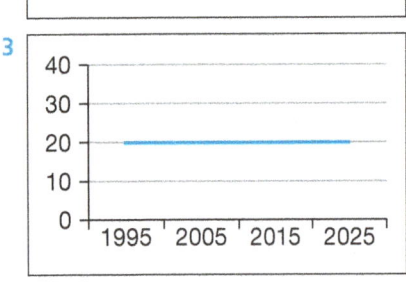
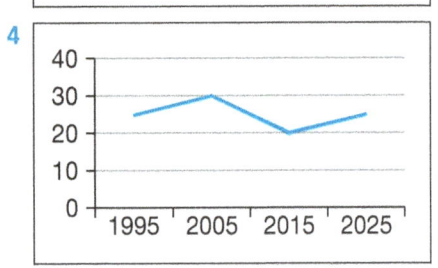

| to increase 1 | to fall | to remain stable | to decrease | to go down |
| to fluctuate | to rise | to drop | to go up | to stay the same |

2. Complete the table with the correct past simple forms of these verbs and any matching nouns.

infinitive	past simple	noun
to increase	increased	1
to rise	2	a rise
to go up	went up	
to decrease	3	a decrease
to fall	fell	4
to go down	5	
to drop	dropped	6
to fluctuate	7	a fluctuation
to remain stable	remained stable	

36 Writing for IELTS

Unit 5

Grammar: Describing trends

You can use adverbs to describe verb changes and adjectives to describe nouns.

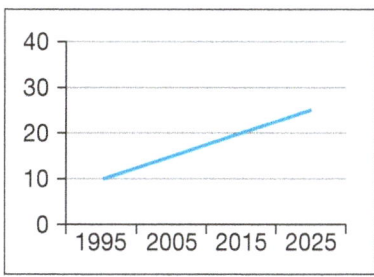

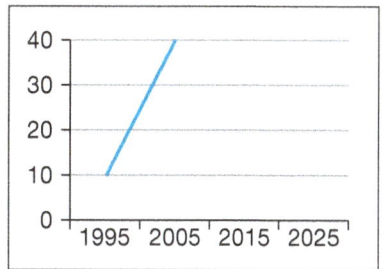

There was + adjective + noun
There was a <u>gradual</u> increase in the number of tourists.

There was + adjective + noun
There was a <u>sharp</u> rise in the number of tourists.

Subject + verb + adverb
The number of tourists increased <u>gradually</u>.

Subject + verb + adverb
The number of tourists rose <u>sharply</u>.

 Watch out

Remember that adjectives come before nouns and adverbs came after verbs:
a rapid (adjective) + *decrease* (noun)
decreased (verb) + *rapidly* (adverb)
Adverbs such as *fast* and *hard* are irregular. (not ~~fastly / hardly~~)

3 Complete the sentences about the graphs. Use suitable adverbs / adjectives if possible.

1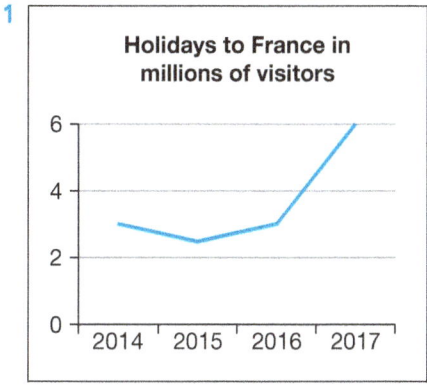

2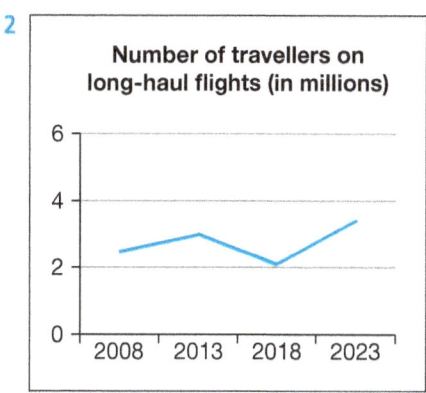

1 There was a <u>*sharp increase*</u> in the number of holidays to France in 2017.
2 The number of travellers on long-haul flights _____ between 2008 and 2023.

Tourism 37

3   Money spent on holidays
    2017 (in thousands of $)

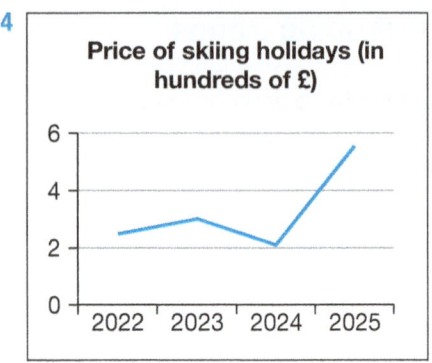

4   Price of skiing holidays (in hundreds of £)

3   There was a _____ in the amount of money spent on holidays in August 2017.
4   The price of skiing holidays _____ in 2025.

Vocabulary: Expressions with time

For Task 1 you may need to use time expressions to explain when something started or finished or to explain when something changed. For example:

from 2008 to 2023   **between** 2014 and 2017   **for** ten years
twenty years **ago**   **in** 2017   **since** 2022   **in** January

4   Complete the time expressions in these sentences describing graphs 1–4 in Exercise 3.

1   There was a slight increase in holidays to France _____ 2014 _____ 2017.
2   The number of long-haul flights fluctuated _____ fifteen years.
3   The money spent on holidays remained stable _____ June and July.
4   The price of skiing holidays rose slightly _____ 2022 to 2023.

Writing for IELTS

Part 2: Skills development

Exam information: Describing line graphs

A line graph shows how the value of something changes over time. The vertical axis shows quantities, e.g. numbers, percentages or money. The horizontal axis shows different points in time, usually months or years. Different quantities measured at different points in time can be joined using a continuous line to show a trend or how these quantities change, e.g. increase, decrease, or stay the same. More lines (different colours or styles) can be used for different categories. The key explains which categories are being measured.

1 Look at the line graph and write T (true) or F (false) next to the sentences below.

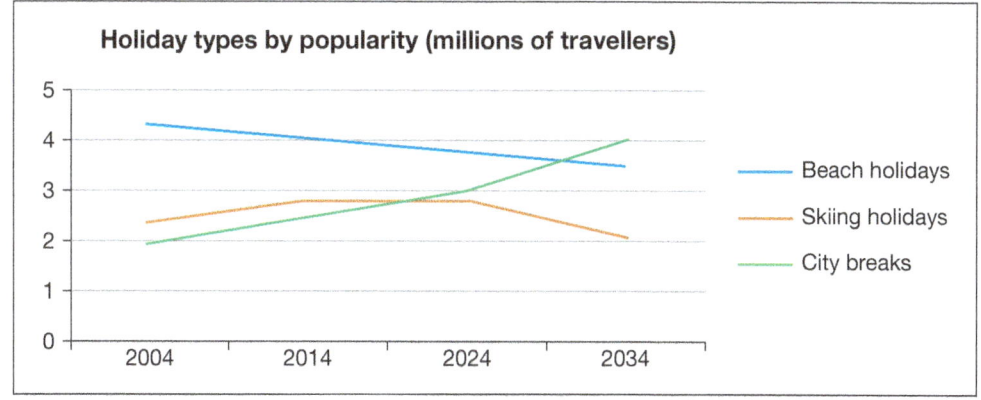

1 The graph shows the popularity of three different types of holiday from 2004 to 2034 in millions of travellers. _T_
2 City breaks increased gradually from 2 million travellers in 2004 to 3 million in 2024. ___
3 There was a slight increase in skiing holidays after 2004, then they remained stable for about 5 years. ___
4 From 2024 to 2034 it is predicted that there will be a sharp rise in the number of people who go on skiing holidays. ___
5 Beach holidays have decreased gradually from over 4 million to 3.5 million travellers. ___
6 From 2014 to 2024 there was a sharp drop in the number of people who went on skiing holidays. ___

Exam tip: Tense

Check the horizontal axis to find the periods of time the graph refers to: past, present, future, or all three.

Use the present simple to describe the graph: *The graph shows …*, *We can see …*

If the graph refers to past periods of time, use the past simple to describe these.

If the graph includes future times, use: *It is predicted that …*, *… will …*

2 Look at the line graph and complete the sentences with the correct forms of the verbs in brackets.

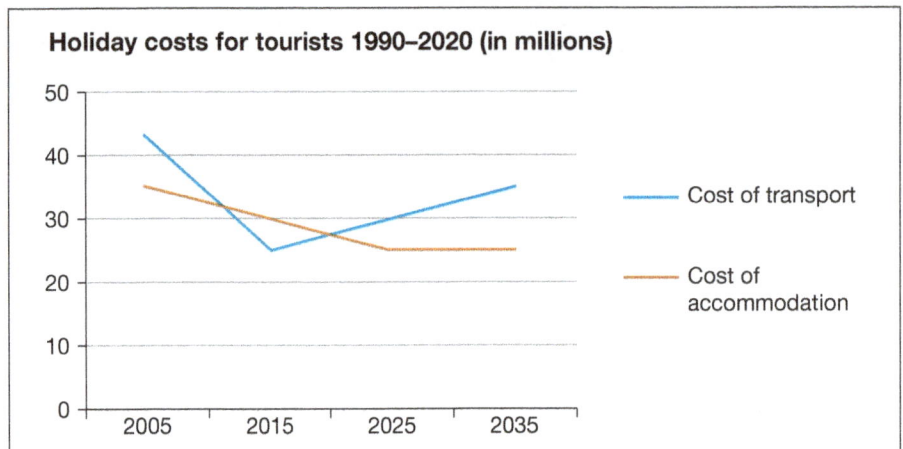

1 The line graph _____ the cost of holidays for tourists from 2005 to 2035. (show)
2 Between 2005 and 2035 the cost of transport _____ rapidly. (drop)
3 The cost of accommodation _____ gradually for thirty years after 1995. (go down)
4 It is predicted that the cost of accommodation _____ from 2025 to 2035. (stay the same)

3 Look at the line graph and complete the text with the correct forms of the verbs in brackets and the correct prepositions.

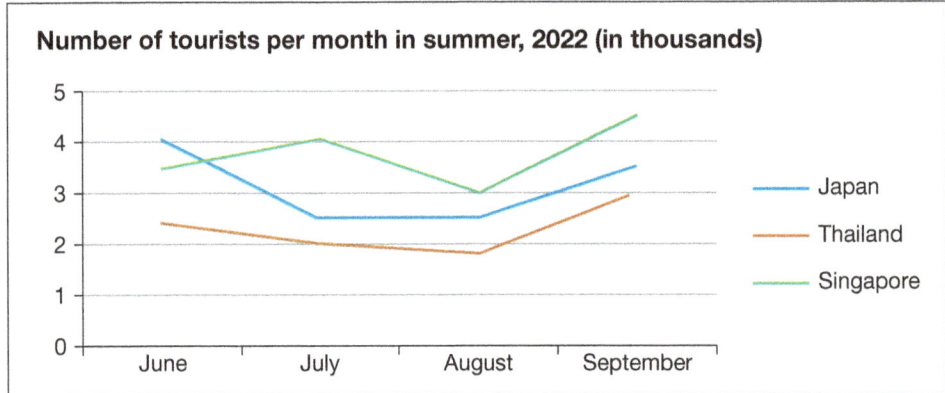

The graph (1) _____ (show) how many tourists (2) _____ (visit) three countries in the summer of 2022. Most tourists (3) _____ (go) to Singapore (4) _____ June and September. The number (5) _____ (fluctuate) between 3.5 and 4.5 thousand. Fewer tourists (6) _____ (travel) to Japan and Thailand. The number of people who visited Thailand (7) _____ (drop) gradually from 2.5 thousand to about 1.8 from June to August then (8) _____ (rise) to 3 thousand (9) _____ September. We can (10) _____ (see) that the trend for Japan (11) _____ (be) similar. There was a sharp drop in tourists from June to July. The number (12) _____ (remain stable) in August and then (13) _____ (increase) steadily in September.

Writing for IELTS

Unit 5

Part 3: Exam practice

Writing Task 1

You should spend about 20 minutes on this task.

The line graph below shows the percentage of tourists to Scotland who visited four different attractions in Edinburgh. Summarize the information by selecting and reporting the main features, and make comparisons where relevant.

Write at least 150 words.

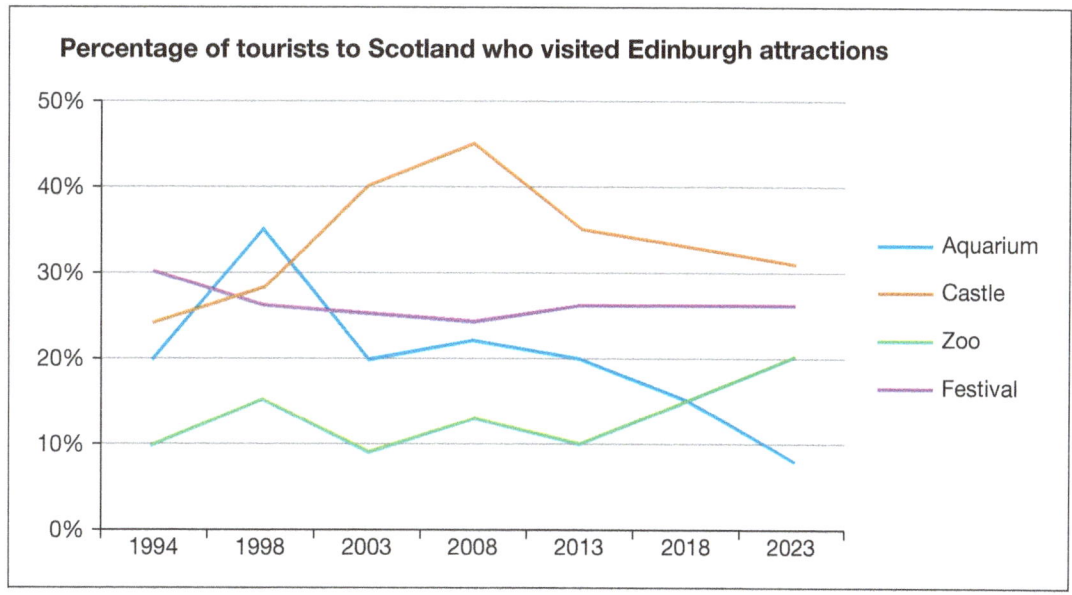

⏩ Progress Check

How many boxes can you tick? You should work towards being able to tick them all.

Did you...
use the correct nouns, verbs, adjectives and adverbs to describe changes in graphs? ☐
use correct word order? ☐
use the correct prepositions with time phrases? ☐
check whether the information in the line graph is about the past, present or future and use the correct tense(s)? ☐

Tourism

6 Films

Language development | Film vocabulary, Percentages and fractions, Approximate amounts
Exam skills | Describing pie charts, Comparing pie charts
Exam practice | Task 1

Part 1: Language development

Vocabulary: Films

1 Complete the types of film to match definitions 1–6.

1 A film that makes people laugh.
   C _omedy_
2 This type of film has a hero as the main character.
   A _ _ _ _ _
3 A factual film about an event or a person.
   D _ _ _ _ _ _ _ _ _
4 A crime or mystery film which is exciting.
   T _ _ _ _ _ _ _
5 A film which makes people afraid.
   H _ _ _ _ _
6 A film based on space and the future. S _ _ _ _ _ _ F _ _ _ _ _ _

2 Circle the correct option.

> In Hollywood famous actors often play the main (1) (character) / personality in a film. The films usually have a (2) chorus / soundtrack to increase the atmosphere. Hollywood films often have a simple (3) history / story and use special (4) effects / factors such as explosions to make the film exciting. Hollywood films can be divided into different (5) genres / topics such as thrillers or romantic films. If films are very successful, they are called (6) movies / blockbusters.

3 Now complete the film descriptions below using words from Exercises 1 and 2.

1 This film is a _____ which tells the true _____ of a woman who lived in Russia in the twentieth century and became a famous film director.
2 *Blackout* is a _____ film set in the twenty-second century. It follows a group of explorers as they visit other planets and try to stay alive. There are lots of _____ such as giant spaceships and explosions.
3 The _____ of film which is most popular with young people is action. They also like film music and often listen to the _____ of films. However, in general young people find _____ films too frightening.

Writing for IELTS

Unit 6

Vocabulary: Percentages and fractions

Percentages (%) and fractions (¼, ⅓, ½, etc.) can both be used to describe proportions of a whole amount.

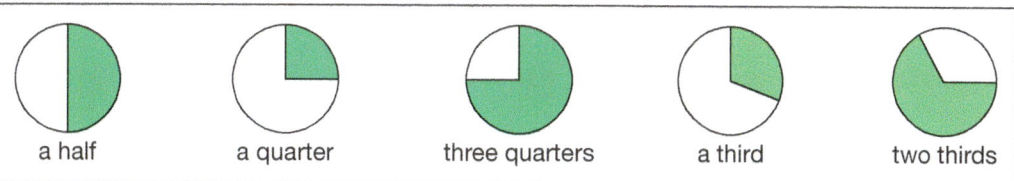

| a half | a quarter | three quarters | a third | two thirds |

4 Match the percentages to the fractions.

50 per cent	25 per cent	75 per cent	33 per cent	66 per cent
two thirds	a half	a third	a quarter	three quarters

> **⚠ Watch out**
>
> *Per cent* is used with a number, e.g. *ten per cent / 50 per cent*
> *Percentage* is used with words, e.g. *the percentage of people / a small percentage of people*

Vocabulary: Expressions with *fraction* and *per cent*

Use these patterns to write about percentages and fractions:

fraction + of + noun + verb   **per cent + of + noun + verb**

A quarter of the people like horror films.   *Ten per cent of boys like action films.*

5 Put the words in the correct order to make sentences.

1 of adults / science fiction / watch / a third / films / do not
2 Bollywood / of worldwide film sales / ten per cent / come from
3 three quarters of / films / on television / people over 65 / watch
4 cartoons / children / on a regular basis / ninety per cent of / watch

Vocabulary: Approximate amounts

If you do not know precise numbers or quantities, you can use words and phrases that express approximate amounts. Look at the bold words in these examples.

About **Approximately**	a third of UK film sales in 2009 were comedy films.
Just under **Almost / Nearly**	a third of UK film sales in 2009 were thrillers.

6 Now match the percentages on the left with the phrases on the right.

1 53 per cent   a just under a quarter
2 30 per cent   b almost all
3 95 per cent   c approximately half
4 23 per cent   d about a third

Films   43

Part 2: Skills development

> **Exam information: Describing pie charts**
> A pie chart is a circle (or 'pie') divided into sections. The whole circle represents the total quantity (= 100%) and the sections show how the total may be divided into different shares or proportions. These shares or proportions correspond to different categories. Pie charts are useful for comparing these categories. Proportions are shown as a percentage (%) or fraction (e.g. ½) of the total quantity.

1 Match sentences 1–6 to pie chart A or B. Write A or B next to each sentence.

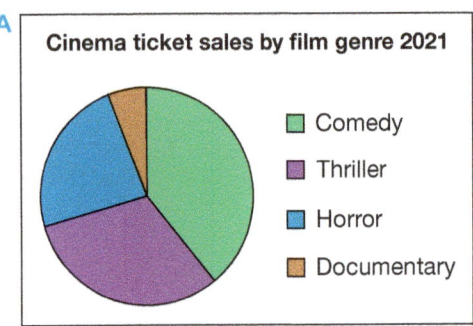
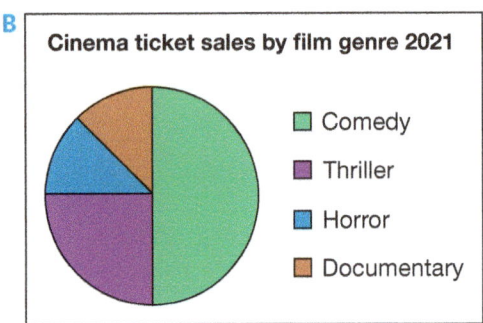

1 Fifty per cent of the cinema tickets sold in 2021 were for comedy films. _B_
2 A third of cinema ticket sales were for comedy films. ___
3 Thrillers were 25 per cent of the total cinema ticket sales in 2021. ___
4 Horror films were about a quarter of cinema ticket sales in the UK in 2021. ___
5 In 2021 comedy films were half the total cinema ticket sales in the UK. ___
6 Less than 10 per cent of cinema tickets sold in the UK in 2021 were documentary films. ___

> **Exam tip: Using approximate language**
> Pie charts often compare different categories in an approximate way. If the sections of the pie chart are not labelled with precise percentages / fractions, you should describe them using approximate language.

2 Write sentences describing the pie chart using the words / phrases in the box.

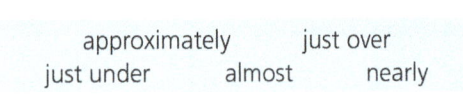

approximately   just over
just under   almost   nearly

Example: *Approximately 10 per cent of cinema visitors are between 40 and 54 years old.*

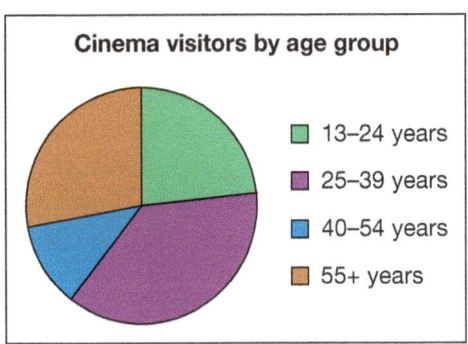

44 Writing for IELTS

Unit 6

ℹ Exam information: Comparing pie charts

For IELTS Task 1 there are sometimes two or three pie charts that you must compare. The pie charts may represent different years and show trends over time. You need to describe the changes and similarities / differences between the pie charts.

3 Look at the pie charts and decide if the sentences below are true or false. Write T (true) or F (false).

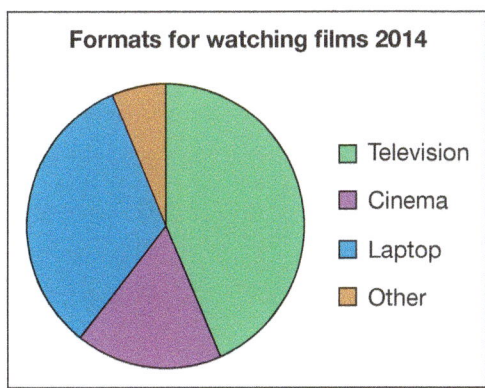
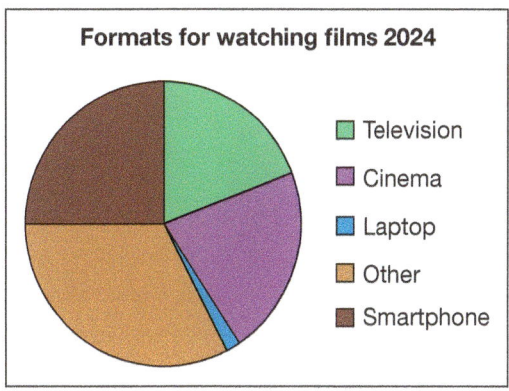

1 The pie charts show how many people watched films in 2014 and 2024. _F_
2 The pie charts show the proportion of films watched on different formats in 2014 and 2024. ___
3 More people watched films on television in 2024 than in 2014. ___
4 In 2014 nearly a third of films were watched on laptops but this amount decreased to about two per cent in 2024. ___
5 The proportion of people watching films at the cinema was about the same in 2014 and 2024. ___
6 There was a slight increase in the number of people watching films on 'other' from 2014 to 2024. ___
7 In 2014 no one used a smartphone to watch films but in 2024 people used a smartphone to watch a quarter of the total films. ___
8 In 2024 approximately half the films were watched using two formats: cinema and smartphones. ___
9 From 2014 to 2024 the number of people watching films on television decreased by just over 25 percent. ___
10 From 2014 to 2024 the number of people watching films on television decreased by approximately half. ___

Films

💡 Exam tip: *By* or *to*?

increase by 10 per cent means that 10% more of a number has been added to it, e.g. 10 + 1 = 11

increase to 10 per cent means a number was less than 10% and is now 10%, e.g. 8% → 10%

4 Complete the text about these pie charts.

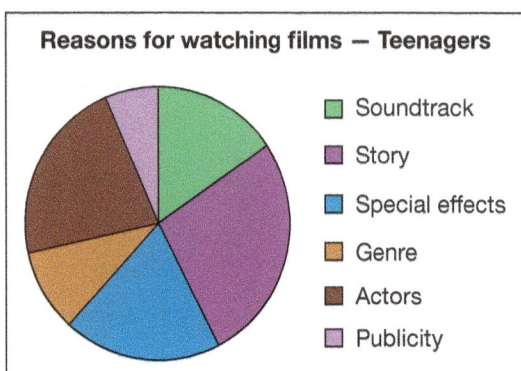 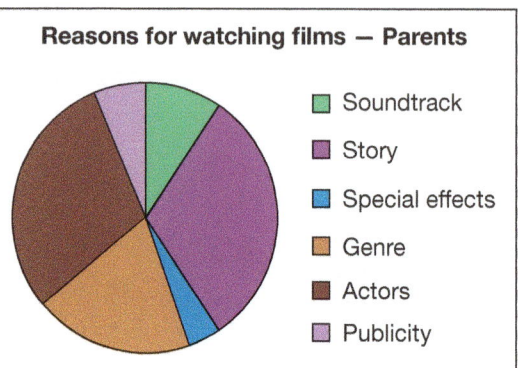

The pie charts show the different reasons why (1) _parents and teenagers_ watch films. In general most people watch films because of the (2) _____ and the actors. The (3) _____ is one of the least important reasons for both groups when they watch films. We can see from the pie chart that almost (4) _____ of teenagers choose films because of the special effects. Another important reason for teenagers is the music at (5) _____ 20 per cent. The reasons for parents are different. (6) _____ of parents choose films for the story and actors; the other reasons are much less important. Special effects are the least important reason for parents at only about (7) _____ .The (8) _____ of teenagers and parents who choose films based on the publicity is (9) _____ the same at about ten (10) _____ .

💡 Exam tip: Words for quantities

Percentage, amount, number, proportion and *quantity* can all be used to describe the quantities shown in graphs and charts in Task 1.

The **percentage** of people who watch horror films decreased.
The **proportion** of people who watched comedies was larger / smaller in 2011 than in 2010.
The **number** of people who prefer action films increased.
Teenagers spend a smaller **amount** / **quantity** on going to the cinema than older people.

Remember: use amount with uncountable nouns only.

Part 3: Exam practice

Writing Task 1

You should spend about 20 minutes on this task.

The pie charts below show the share of Oscar winners by film genre for 2013 and 2023. Summarize the information by selecting and reporting the main features, and make comparisons where relevant.

Write at least 150 words.

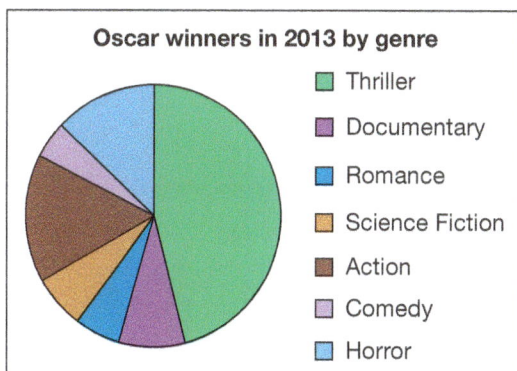

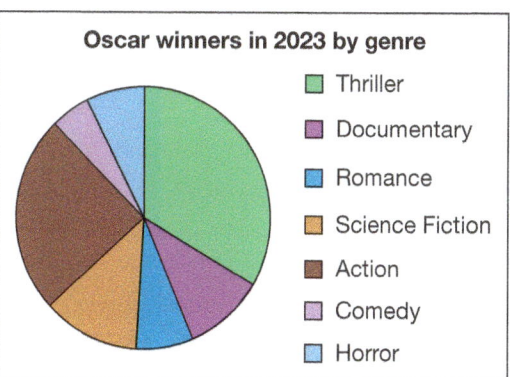

Progress Check

How many boxes can you tick? You should work towards being able to tick them all.

Did you...
use percentages and fractions to describe quantities? ☐
use correct word order: fraction / percentage + of + noun + verb? ☐
describe the pie chart accurately if precise percentages / fractions are given or use approximate expressions if necessary? ☐
describe any similarities and differences between two pie charts? ☐

Review 2

1 Correct the underlined parts of these sentences.

1. A <u>comedy</u> is a film that scares people.
2. The number of radio listeners is increasing <u>slow</u>.
3. Children <u>shouldn't to be</u> rude to older people.
4. Seventy-five per cent of people is <u>a half</u>.
5. You <u>don't need to</u> break laws.
6. There was a <u>drop sharp</u> in the number of people watching documentaries.

2 Add sentences a–d to the essay paragraphs below by writing a, b, c or d in the gaps, then number the paragraphs in order 1–4.

a. These are the main reasons why tourism can be just as negative as positive.
b. Firstly, when an area becomes a tourist destination, it can lose some of its traditional ways.
c. I believe tourism is just as negative as it is positive because tourism can damage local culture and be bad for the environment.
d. Tourism is also bad for the environment in general.

Tourism does as much damage to a place as good. Do you agree or disagree with this statement? Give reasons for your answer.

A: _____ Busy tourist resorts can get a lot of litter, and a place that was once beautiful can become quite ugly because of this. On a larger scale, travelling long distances by air can be damaging for the planet because it creates a lot of pollution. ☐

B: Tourism has increased dramatically over the last thirty years because of easier and cheaper air travel, meaning more and more people can get to other places quickly and easily. Many people see tourism as a good thing for countries, but tourism also has many negative aspects. _____ ☐

C: _____ People need to think about the environment and local culture before they travel abroad on holiday. If these things aren't considered, some areas could be badly affected. ☐

D: _____ For example, tourists come and often signs are put up in foreign languages. In many tourist resorts there are bars, shops and staff that do not represent the local culture. Sometimes, a person can go on holiday and not hear the local language at all. It is important to preserve local languages and customs or they may be lost. ☐

3 Complete the text about this line graph using the phrases from the box. (Put references i–vii in the correct gaps.)

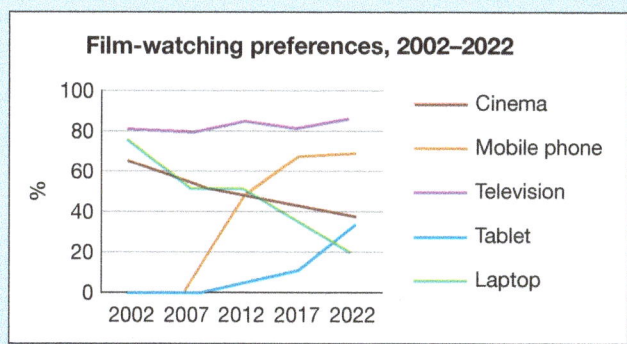

The line graph shows how people liked to watch films between 2002 and 2022. We can see that some methods of watching films became less popular, while some other newer methods became very popular. We can also see that watching films on television has always stayed popular.

Firstly, both laptops and cinema _____ . Watching on laptops _____ . This is similar to watching films at cinemas, which _____ .

Some methods of watching films have become more popular. Watching films on tablets and on mobile phones both _____ . There was a _____ (from 0% to 65%) in watching films on mobile phones. Watching films on tablets _____ to just under 40%. The high percentage of people who watched films on television _____ at around 80%.

i	rose steadily from 0%	v	fell steadily by about 20% over this time
ii	dropped from nearly 80% in 1985 to around 20% in 2005	vi	decreased steadily over the twenty year period
iii	increased from 1990 to 2005	vii	sharp rise
iv	remained stable		

4 Look at the pie chart and write T (true) or F (false) after each sentence below.

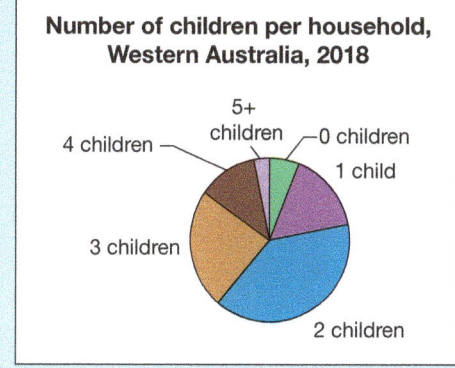

1 About two thirds of families had two or three children. ___
2 Half of all families had two children. ___
3 The smallest proportion is families with five or more children. ___
4 About a third of families had either one or no children, or four children or more. ___
5 Around a quarter of families had three children ___
6 People with no children were the smallest group. ___

7 Technology

Language development | Technology vocabulary, Agreement linking words
Exam skills | Contrast linking words
Exam practice | Task 2 Advantage and disadvantage essay

Part 1: Language development

Vocabulary: Technology

1 Match pictures a–f to labels 1–6.

a

b

c

d

e

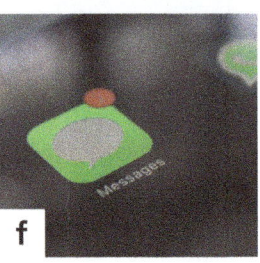
f

1 streaming music   d
2 texting
3 emailing
4 using social media
5 video calling
6 playing a video game

Vocabulary: Agreement linking words

To connect two agreeing ideas we can use linking words such as: in addition, moreover, furthermore and also. Look at the examples:

Idea 1	Linking word	Agreeing idea
Computers give students access to lots of information.	**In addition, Moreover, Furthermore, Also,**	computers make studying more time effective.

We can also add an example using *for example*:

Computers give students access to lots of information. ***For example****, there are dictionaries and reference books online.*

Writing for IELTS

Unit 7

2 Look at the essay questions and complete each sentence below with an agreeing idea.

1 *Why is playing video games bad for children?*
Playing video games can be bad for children's eyes. In addition, _____

2 *How can technology help us at work?*
Technology at work makes it easier to communicate with other companies. Furthermore, _____

3 *How can social media be negative?*
Social media can be a waste of time. Also, _____

Vocabulary: Contrast linking words

To contrast ideas, we can use linking words such as however, yet, although and on the other hand. Look at the examples:

Idea 1	Linking word	Contrasting idea
Computers give students access to lots of information.	However, On the other hand,	not all information online is correct.
Computers give students access to lots of information,	yet although	not all information online is correct.

3 Look at the essay questions and complete each sentence below with a contrasting idea.

1 *Why is playing video games bad for children?*
Playing video games can be bad for children's eyes, yet _____

2 *How can technology help us at work?*
Technology makes it easier to communicate with other companies. However, _____

3 *How can social media be negative?*
Social media can be a waste of time for some people. On the other hand, _____

> ⚠️ **Watch out**
>
> Remember that some linking words (e.g. However) must start a new sentence after a comma and some linking words join two clauses within one sentence (e.g. although).
>
> *I like mobile phones, however I don't like texting.* ✗
> *I like mobile phones. However, I don't like texting.* ✓
>
> *I like mobile phones. Although I don't like texting.* ✗
> *I like mobile phones, although I don't like texting.* ✓

4 Correct the mistakes in these texts.

1 Technology is a good thing because it helps people communicate more easily also it helps people do their jobs more efficiently.

2 People should always pay for music and not download it illegally. Downloading illegally is bad for the music industry. In addition, musicians.

3 Computers have some negative points. It is not always easy to fix a computer if it goes wrong. In addition, there are lots of people who can fix computers.

4 Mobile phones can be dangerous if they are used in a car. However, they can be dangerous for pedestrians who use them when crossing the road.

Technology   51

Part 2: Skills development

> **Exam information: Advantage and disadvantage essays**
> For a Task 2 essay, you may have to evaluate questions or arguments. To do this, you will need to consider their advantages and disadvantages in a balanced way to show that you understand both sides.

1 Read the list of ideas for the essay question below and decide if they are advantages or disadvantages. Write A (advantage) or D (disadvantage) next to each idea.

What are the advantages and disadvantages of children using smartphones?

1 Parents can easily contact their children. *A*
2 The charges for using data on smartphones can be very expensive. ___
3 Children spend too much time texting their friends on smartphones. ___
4 Smartphones are often lost or stolen. ___
5 Children can use smartphones as cameras and music players. ___
6 Smartphones distract children from studying. ___
7 Children always have a way of contacting their parents in an emergency. ___
8 There are many ways smartphones can help children learn. ___

2 Match the supporting information on the right to the ideas from Exercise 1 on the left.

Ideas		Supporting information	
1	Parents can easily contact their children.	a	Some parents cannot afford to pay smartphone charges.
2	The charges for talking on smartphones are very expensive.	b	It is expensive to replace them.
3	Children spend too much time talking to their friends on smartphones.	c	They do not need to buy other types of technology
4	Smartphones are often lost or stolen.	d	They should focus on their school work.
5	Smartphones distract children from studying.	e	This can stop parents worrying about where their children are.
6	Children can use smartphones as cameras and music players.	f	They should spend less time chatting and more time doing other activities.
7	Children have a way of contacting their parents in an emergency.	g	For example, they can learn through playing games.
8	There are many ways smartphones can help children learn.	h	This could help if children have accidents.

Writing for IELTS

3 Match ideas a–f to paragraph functions 1–6.

1 Main idea — e
2 Example
3 Reason
4 Expansion
5 Supporting idea 1
6 Supporting idea 2

a Today, these phones are used by most people to keep in contact with friends and work.
b Mobile phones can help parents find out where their children are.
c For example, if a child is not home on time, their parents can call them and check where they are.
d In addition, mobile phones make arrangements easier.
e Mobile phones are an excellent tool for communication.
f This is because people can use their mobile phones to change plans or call people if they are delayed.

4 Now decide the best order for sentences a–f in a paragraph and write it here:

e __ __ __ __ __

> **Exam tip: Organizing an essay**
> One way of organizing an essay about advantages and disadvantages is to write one paragraph giving the advantages of an argument / solution and one paragraph giving the disadvantages.

5 Read the essay question and the ideas below, then put the ideas into two groups: advantages and disadvantages.

What are the advantages and disadvantages of social media?

1 Sometimes people think they are talking to someone they know, but it might be a stranger.
2 Social media means we can keep in touch with friends and family easily.
3 If a person has relatives in another country, they can keep in contact using social media.
4 Social media can be addictive, especially in young people.
5 Social media helps people pass on news.
6 Young people may spend too much time on social media compared to other activities.
7 Often when a news story breaks, social media help us hear the experiences and opinions of the people where the news is happening.
8 Nobody knows the true identity of some of the people using social media.

6 Use the ideas from Exercise 4 to write two paragraphs, one paragraph about advantages and one about disadvantages. Begin your paragraphs like this:

There are many advantages of social media. Firstly, …

However, social media also has some disadvantages. …

> **Exam tip: Ordering ideas**
> Remember to order your ideas in a logical way and use linking words (*However, On the other hand, In addition, Furthermore*, etc.) to show how your ideas are connected.

7 Write short notes listing advantages and disadvantages for each of the essay titles below.

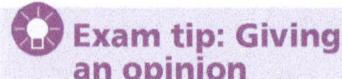

Exam tip: Giving an opinion

When you have described the advantages and disadvantages of a situation / argument, you can say which side has the strongest case in your opinion.

1 What are the advantages and disadvantages of watching TV and streaming shows?
2 There are more advantages than disadvantages of modern technology. How far do you agree with this statement?
3 The internet has more advantages for young people than old people. Do you agree?

8 Read the following essay about using social media at work and complete paragraph 3 with your own ideas, including reasons and examples.

What are the advantages and disadvantages of using social media in the workplace?

Social media is common nowadays. There are few people who don't have an account on platforms like Instagram, Facebook or TikTok. However, whether people should use them at work is debatable. Some people say that these platforms should be banned at work, while others say that they can be an advantage. I believe social media should be allowed in the workplace.

Firstly, many people say social media should be banned in a work environment because staff spend too much time using it when they should be working and this can have a negative effect on a company's productivity. People use these platforms at work in order to keep up-to-date with news and gossip. However, many people have lost their jobs because they have used social media too frequently or because they have said something negative about their company or their bosses on such platforms.

On the other hand, these platforms can also have advantages in the workplace. _____
_____
_____
_____
_____
_____
_____

In conclusion, I believe that, although there are disadvantages to using social media in the workplace, people should be able to do it.

Part 3: Exam practice

Writing Task 2

You should spend about 40 minutes on this task.

Write about the following topic:

> *Shopping online has as many disadvantages as it does advantages.*
> *To what extent do you agree with this statement?*

Give reasons for your answer and include any relevant examples from your own knowledge or experience.

Write at least 250 words.

Progress Check

How many boxes can you tick? You should work towards being able to tick them all.

Did you...
- use linking words to connect agreeing and contrasting ideas? ☐
- describe both the advantages and the disadvantages of an idea / argument / proposal? ☐
- give examples and reasons for the advantages and disadvantages? ☐
- give your own opinion about whether the advantages or disadvantages are stronger? ☐

8 Happiness

Language development | Money vocabulary, Pronouns for referencing
Exam skills | Agreeing and contrasting opinions
Exam practice | Task 2 essay giving opinions

Part 1: Language development

Vocabulary: Money

1 Decide if the words in the box below are nouns, verbs or adjectives. Write N, V or A next to each word. (One word can have two labels.) Then match the words to the definitions.

wealth	spend
save	rich A
possessions	inherit
salary	tax
poverty	wealthy
savings	income

1 Money that the government takes from you __tax__
2 Money that you keep for the future _____
3 Money you receive from your employer _____
4 The noun for being poor _____
5 An adjective to describe rich people _____
6 Money you receive from work, rent or investments _____
7 Things that you own _____

2 Complete Fariba's speech bubble with words from Exercise 1.

Fariba

In my country people do not pay much money to the government in (1) _____ . In general most people earn a good (2) _____ from their jobs and we make sure we (3) _____ enough money for the future. Some people are (4) _____ and live in large houses and own expensive cars. These people (5) _____ a lot of money on possessions. Some of their (6) _____ comes from renting flats to other people and from business investments.

Grammar: Pronouns *it, they* and *this*

Pronouns are used to refer to nouns that have already been mentioned. Using pronouns helps you avoid repetition, connects your sentences together and makes your writing more fluent.

Money is necessary to live. It pays for accommodation, food and clothing. (It = money)
People who do not have a lot of money can be happy. They can be happy for other reasons.
(They = people who do not have a lot of money)

You can use *this* to refer to whole ideas:

The number of wealthy people is increasing in some parts of the world. This is good for the economy. (This = The number of wealthy people is increasing in some parts of the world)

3 Complete the sentences below using *it*, *they* or *this*.

1 People who enjoy their work are often happy. ___This___ means they often work harder and are better employees.
2 Happiness comes in many different forms. For some people _____ comes from work. For others _____ comes from enjoying life.
3 The main reason people want to earn money is to improve their life. For example, _____ might want to have more possessions.
4 Good weather can have an effect on people's happiness. _____ makes them feel more positive and less stressed.
5 Children often make a couple happier. _____ help adults focus on the most important things in life.
6 People who inherit a lot from their parents can become wealthy overnight. _____ makes their lives much easier because _____ no longer have to worry about their future income.

4 Now underline the noun or idea that each pronoun refers to. (The first one has been done as an example.)

Grammar: Pronouns *this/that* + noun

Sometimes we use this / these + noun to refer to an idea / different ideas.

People who have a negative attitude to life can be very unhappy. **This problem** *can affect everyone.*

Taxes have increased, salaries have been cut and food prices have risen. **These factors** *have led to a drop in living standards across the region*

5 Complete the sentences with this or these and a suitable noun (singular or plural) from the box.

| approach | action | problem | change |

1 When governments raise or lower taxes, the income of citizens can increase or decrease. _____ _____ affect a whole nation for many years.
2 Talking about money problems can help people understand how to manage them better in the future. _____ _____ is often used by counsellors.
3 Giving advice or gifts and lending money to friends are common in all cultures. _____ _____ help to increase the bonds between people.
4 It is difficult to know how much money to save for the future. _____ _____ is common for many families with children.

6 Now underline the verbs after the added nouns. Are they singular or plural? Write S or P next to sentences 1–4 above.

> ⚠️ **Watch out**
>
> Make sure nouns, pronouns and verbs agree in number with the nouns they refer back to.

Part 2: Skills development

 Exam information: Giving opinions

For a Task 2 essay you will often be asked to give your own opinion. You should also include a range of other viewpoints to show that you understand both sides of an argument.

To give your own opinion, use phrases such as *In my view / opinion* and verb phrases such as *I think that / I believe that ... .*

To show other people's opinions, use *According to* + group of people (e.g. *parents / scientists / politicians*) ... .

Use verb phrases such as *Some people think that / Many people believe that / People argue that / Other people claim that ... .*

Other verbs include *suggest / state / say*.

1 Read the sentences and decide if they are the writer's opinion or the opinion of other people. Write WO (writer's opinion) or OPO (other people's opinion).

   1 According to the government, traditional families are the happiest.
   2 There are many things that can make people happy. In my view, family and friends are the most important.
   3 Some teachers believe that children should learn how to manage money at school. They suggest that this could help the economy in the future.
   4 I believe that the government should provide more financial help to poor families.
   5 My personal opinion is that having an enjoyable job is essential for happiness.
   6 Many people argue that all citizens should pay as little tax as possible.
   7 I think that wealthy people should pay more tax.
   8 Parents often claim that they need more money.

2 Now underline the phrases which introduce each opinion in sentences 1–8 above.

3 Read the introduction to the essay below and underline the phrases used to introduce the writer's opinion and the opinions of other people.

 **Exam tip: Your opinion**

For Task 2 you should say briefly what your own opinion is in the introduction to your essay so that this is clear from the start.

> *If people have more money, they are generally happier.* To what extent do you agree with this statement?
>
> Money is important in life but it does not always bring happiness. Some people say that having more money makes life less stressful, while other people argue that happiness can be found in other aspects of life such as work, family or hobbies. In my view, having more money does not make people happier but it makes life easier. There are two reasons for my opinion.

4 Answer these questions about the introduction.

1 What do some people say? ....
2 What do other people argue? ....
3 What does the writer think? ....
4 How many reasons will the writer give for his / her opinion? ....

5 Write an introduction for the following essay title. Remember to give your opinion and introduce the opinions of other people. Use your own ideas and the notes in the box to help you.

Personal happiness comes from being successful in life. How far do you agree with this statement?

happiness comes from:
positive attitude to life
being famous
success in job

religion
having lots of friends
life experiences — holidays, sports, hobbies
possessions — house, car, clothes

☀ Exam tip: Agreeing and contrasting opinions

Use the main body of your essay to explain your opinion and agree or disagree with the opinions of other people. Use linking words such as in addition, similarly and also when describing ideas connected to one viewpoint, and use however, yet, on the other hand, and although to introduce contrasting points.

6 Complete this paragraph for the essay in Exercise 2 using suitable linking words. (Think about whether each sentence or clause agrees or contrasts with what has just been said.)

Firstly, I believe that money makes life easier because it reduces stress and worry. Families who have enough money to spend on accommodation, food and clothing are less stressed and so have fewer arguments. (1) _____, children from wealthy families often do better at school, (2) _____ this may be because they can afford to pay for good schools. (3) _____, some people think that money cannot solve all family problems. (4) _____ they believe that love from parents is more important than money for bringing up children. (5) _____, I think that it can be difficult for parents to be positive and loving if they are always worrying about money.

7 Now continue this paragraph giving your own opinions and the opinions of other people. Use the notes in the box and add your own notes. Remember to use linking words correctly.

> Secondly, having more money can help people plan for the future so they have more control over their lives. …

Saving money for children's education – children have better future
Getting a better job increases income – can buy more possessions – better life
Saving money for old age – less need to ask others for financial help

Your ideas:

8 Complete the following paragraph with suitable referencing words, e.g. pronouns, this and that and linking words.

> **Happiness is considered very important in life.** What are the best ways to be happy?

One of the best ways to be happy is to try to develop a positive attitude to life. In my opinion, (1) _____ approach can help people to reduce stress and negative feelings. (2) _____ can be much happier simply by thinking about all the good things in their life: family, friends, good health and pets. They can (3) _____ focus on improving things they are less happy about such as getting a better job or moving to a new place. (4) _____, many other people say that (5) _____ isn't easy for people who have serious money problems or no chance of changing their life. (6) _____ factors can often cause people to have problems with stress and ill health. (7) _____ problems can affect how happy someone is (8) _____ staying positive can still help in these situations.

9 Now write another paragraph for this essay question.

60 Writing for IELTS

Part 3: Exam practice

Writing Task 2

You should spend about 40 minutes on this task.

Write about the following topic:

Friends and family bring more happiness than money and possessions. How far do you agree with this statement?

Give reasons for your answer and include any relevant examples from your own knowledge or experience.

Write at least 250 words.

➡ Progress Check

How many boxes can you tick? You should work towards being able to tick them all.

Did you...
- use reference words to connect ideas and avoid repetition? ☐
- use opinion verbs and phrases to introduce your opinions and the opinions of other people? ☐
- use linking words to introduce agreeing and contrasting sentences / clauses? ☐
- check that nouns, pronouns and verbs agree, i.e. singular and plural? ☐

9 The natural world

Language development | Changing environment, The passive
Exam skills | Showing the order of stages
Exam practice | Task 1 Describing a process

Part 1: Language development

Vocabulary: Changing environment

1 Match the words to their definitions.

1	volcano	*e*	A the mixture of gases around the earth.
2	acid rain		B a large river of ice which moves slowly.
3	glacier		C damage caused to nature by chemicals or waste.
4	pollution		D the measurement of heat or cold.
5	atmosphere		E a mountain with a hole on the top where red lava comes out.
6	temperature		F rain which contains large amounts of harmful chemicals.

2 Now complete the sentences with the correct forms of the words from Exercise 1.

1 In summer it can be very hot here; the _____ can reach 40°.
2 The plants were destroyed by _____ from the factory.
3 The _____ erupted and lava started to flow down the mountain.

Grammar: The passive

We can use the passive to describe a process. We use the passive for the following reasons:

1 When who or what did the action (= the agent) is not known
2 When who or what did the action is not important
3 When we want to focus on the object of the action more than the subject

Passive = *Volcanoes are formed by the movement of the Earth's surface.*
Active = *The movement of the Earth's surface forms volcanoes.*

Passive = *Bananas are grown in hot climates.*
Active = *People grow bananas in hot climates.*

We form the passive with the verb *to be* + past participle.
Sometimes an agent with *by* is included: *Seeds are planted by farmers.*
Sometimes there is no agent: *Seeds are planted in the fields.*

3 Number the phrases in the box 1–6 to describe the stages in a plant's life.

plants grow   flowers are picked   plants are watered
seeds are planted **/**   plants die   plants flower

4 Complete the sentences using present simple passive forms of the verbs in brackets.
1 Water ____*is stored*____ (store) in reservoirs and used in the fields.
2 Grass _____ (eat) by cows and cows _____ (eat) by people.
3 Many buildings _____ (destroy) by bad storms in winter.
4 Rainforests _____ (inhabit) by thousands of plants and insects.
5 Forests _____ (damage) by acid rain from factories.
6 Most pollution _____ (cause) by human activity.

5 Correct the errors in the passive in these sentences.
1 In many countries birds ~~is~~ *are* fed by people in the winter.
2 Chemicals are used farmers to protect plants from insects.
3 Seeds are plant in the spring.
4 Elephants and camels used as working animals in some countries.
5 Volcanoes and other natural disasters is studied by scientists.
6 Fields be watered by a special system called irrigation.

> ⚠️ **Watch out**
>
> Verbs that are intransitive (a verb without an object in the active) cannot be used in the passive. e.g. heat rises NOT heat is risen

The natural world   **63**

Part 2: Skills development

> **Exam information: Describing a process**
> For IELTS Task 1 you may have to describe a physical process. This may be illustrated in the form of a diagram showing the different steps or stages in the process. In a process description some verbs will be in the passive and some in the active.

1 Look at the diagram below and put the sentences in the correct order, 1–8.

- a The pollution is carried to the sea by rivers.
- b Pollution is stored in clouds and falls as acid rain.
- c Sea life and fish are killed by polluted water.
- d Factories produce gas pollution and liquid pollution.
- e Gas pollution rises into the air.
- f Liquid pollution is also produced by factories.
- g This acid rain can damage plants and animals in the countryside.
- h Liquid pollution is pumped into nearby rivers.

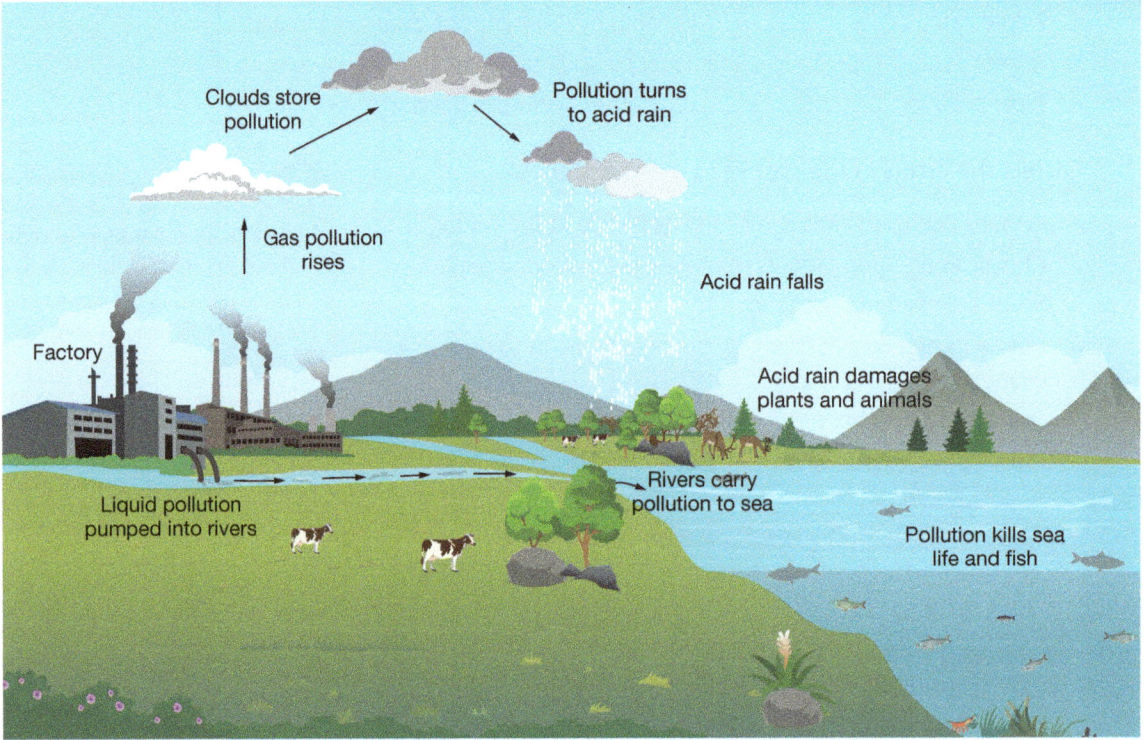

Unit 9

🔆 Exam tip: Expanding Labels

For this task type, the labels on the diagram are in note form. You will need to use this information and expand the information.

Sometimes the label will just be a noun e.g. *factory*. Other times, words will be missing in the labels. e.g.

Liquid pollution (is) pumped into rivers.

Rivers carry pollution to (the) sea.

These notes can be expanded in your writing. e.g. Factories along the river create pollution, and this pollution is then pumped into the rivers. These rivers carry the pollution out to the sea.

2 Look at the diagram below and use the labels and the notes below to write full sentences.

1 during / eruption / magma rises / volcano's main vent
   During an eruption magma rises up the volcano's main vent.
2 magma / erupt from / crater / top / volcano
3 magma / change into / lava
4 ash cloud / form / above / volcano
5 lava flows down / side / volcano
6 many trees / killed / lava

The natural world   65

> ### 🔆 Exam tip: Showing the order of stages
>
> The first sentence of a process description should explain what the diagram shows.
>
> To show the order of stages, use sequence adverbs:
>
> Use *first, firstly* or *first of all* for the first stage.
> Use *secondly / next / then / and then* to describe each of the following stages.
> Use *finally* for the last stage.
>
> You can also use clauses with *when* or *after* to show sequence:
> **When** the apples are ripe, they are picked and packed into boxes.
> **After** the wheat is harvested, it is taken to the barn.

3 Look at the diagram below. Complete the text with words showing sequence from the Exam tip box.

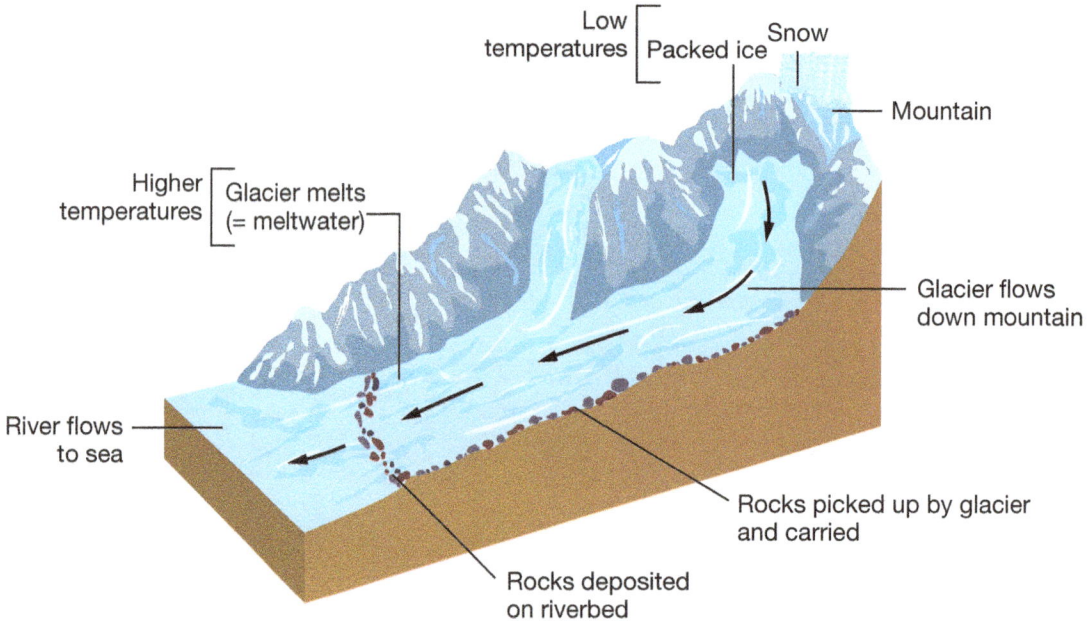

This diagram shows how a glacier is formed and how it moves and changes. (1) _____ a large amount of snow falls on the top of a mountain. Because the temperature at the top of the mountain is very low, this snow never melts. (2) _____ more snow falls on top of it, the snow turns to ice. Eventually, a lot of ice is packed together, and (3) _____ it forms a glacier. The glacier becomes very heavy and it starts to move slowly down the mountain.

4 Now write more sentences to describe the rest of the process. Remember to include some active and some passive verbs.

Unit 9

Part 3: Exam practice

Writing Task 1

You should spend about 20 minutes on this task.

The diagram shows the process of making wheat. Describe the process.

Write at least 150 words.

(a) Plant seeds

(b) 4-8 months

(c) Plants cut

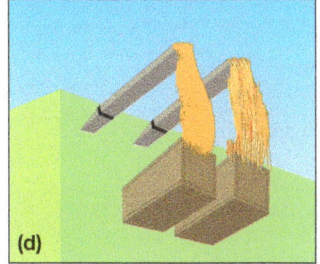
(d) Separate wheat and straw

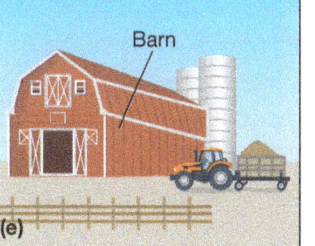
(e) Store wheat

(f) straw put in bales   left in field

(g) Transported to factory

(h) Processed into flour

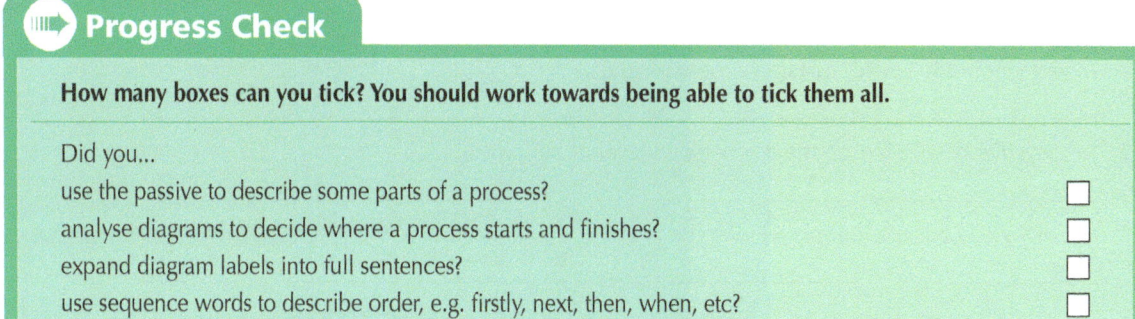

> **Progress Check**
>
> **How many boxes can you tick? You should work towards being able to tick them all.**
>
> Did you...
> use the passive to describe some parts of a process? ☐
> analyse diagrams to decide where a process starts and finishes? ☐
> expand diagram labels into full sentences? ☐
> use sequence words to describe order, e.g. firstly, next, then, when, etc? ☐

The natural world

Review 3

1 Correct the underlined words.

1 People who have a lot of money are <u>wealth</u>.
2 <u>Poverty</u> people cannot buy all the things they want.
3 One in 10 people live within the danger range of an active <u>vulcano</u>.
4 People can get more money by increasing their monthly <u>save</u>.
5 A lot of young people <u>unload</u> music onto their smartphones.
6 <u>Society</u> media is popular all over the world.
7 Smoke from factories and cars pollutes the <u>atmospheer</u>.
8 <u>Radiate</u> is bad for our health.

2 Complete the sentences below with the correct reference word (*it, they, this* or *these*).

1 Having a good job brings happiness to many people because _____ feel that their life is important.
2 Some companies contribute to polluting the environment. _____ is a problem that governments should focus on.
3 Technological advances have helped in medicine, communication and travel. _____ improvements have made a big difference to our lives.
4 Happiness has different meanings for people but _____ is something that is important for everyone.
5 In winter, storms can cause serious damage to shops, offices and houses. Engineers should make _____ buildings stronger.
6 The mountain climbers reached the summit after three weeks. _____ were happy but exhausted.

3 Rewrite the sentences below using the passive.

1 Social media platforms create new ways of communicating.
   _____
2 Farmers keep animals in fields during the day.
   _____
3 Online businesses protect people's personal information.
   _____
4 Movement in the Earth's surface causes volcanos.
   _____
5 Money, friends and family affect a person's level of happiness.
   _____
6 Social media connects people all over the world.
   _____

4 Number the sentences in the correct order 1–7 to make a paragraph comparing online shopping with shopping at a shopping centre.

  a They worry that their credit card details might be copied or that someone might steal money from their bank account. ☐

  b For example, car parking and travelling by train or bus costs money. ☐

  c Some people think that online shopping is much better than going to a shopping centre. ☐

  d In addition, you may not find the products you want in the shops. ☐

  e The internet, on the other hand, gives you freedom to look at lots of shops quickly and find out if the product you want is available. ☐

  f This is because when you go to a shopping centre, you have to pay to get there. ☐

  g However, other people think that shopping on the internet is not secure. ☐

5 Rewrite the text, adding link words, opinion phrases and reference words.

Some people think that money has a negative effect on society and cannot make people happy. Some people think that money has a positive effect on society and can make people happy. Money has positive and negative effects on happiness for the following reasons.

If we do not have money, life is difficult. If we have enough money, life is easier. Wealthy people worry less. Poor people worry more. Other things in life can make people happy. Hobbies and sports make people happy. When you have hobbies and do sports, you meet people and enjoy life. It can be better than having lots of money.

6 Look at the life cycle of a butterfly. Circle the correct option in each sentence, then number sentences a–d in the correct order 1–4.

  a When it is the right size, the caterpillar grows a hard skin called a pupa. Inside the pupa the caterpillar *loses / is lost* its old body parts and grows completely new ones, including wings. ☐

  b A butterfly starts life as a small round egg. This egg *lay / is laid* on the leaves of plants. ☐

  c Finally, the butterfly *releases / is released*. After some time, it will fly away to begin its adult life and start the cycle again. ☐

  d When the egg hatches, a caterpillar *emerges / is emerged*. The caterpillar has to eat as much as possible in order to grow. ☐

Review 69

10 Places to live

Language development | Public spaces, Describing change, Comparatives and Superlatives, Present Perfect
Exam skills | Comparing more than one visual, main trends
Exam practice | Task 1 Comparing more than one visual

Part 1: Language development

Vocabulary: Public spaces

1 Match the words in the box to the pictures.

> shopping centre   industrial area   residential area
> entertainment complex   sports centre   business park

1 _residential area_

2 _____

3 _____

4 _____

5 _____

6 _____

Vocabulary: Describing change

2 Match words 1–8 to their definitions a–h.

1 To improve	c	a	to become larger
2 To expand	☐	b	to make something smaller
3 To reduce something	☐	c	to become better
4 To convert something	☐	d	to increase in size or number
5 To transform something	☐	e	to change the form or purpose of something
6 To grow	☐	f	to change something completely

70   Writing for IELTS

Unit 10

Grammar: Present Perfect

We use the present perfect to describe recent changes in the past that are still continuing now or are still relevant now.

The present perfect is formed as follows: has / have + past participle.

*The sports centres **have improved** because the local government spent a lot of money on them.*
*The business centre of our town **has expanded** over the last ten years.*

3 Complete the sentences with the present perfect form of the verbs in brackets.

1 Residential areas around London ___*have grown*___ (grow) because more people want to live near the city.
2 Fast-food restaurants across the world _____ (transform) the way people eat in towns and cities.
3 A property company _____ (convert) many old factories into new offices.
4 Since the new entertainment complex opened, life in the town _____ (improve).
5 The shopping centre _____ (expand) recently and now has more clothes shops.
6 New traffic regulations _____ (reduce) the number of cars in the city.

Grammar: Comparatives and Superlatives

Look at the examples of comparative and superlative adjective forms.

*The population of Summerville was the **highest** in 2010*
*The average house price was **higher** in 2010 **than** in 2005.*

4 Look at the information about the town of Summerville in the table and circle the correct options in the sentences below.

Changes in Summerville 2015-2023			
	2015	2019	2023
Average house prices	$150,000	$155,000	$159,000
Population	45,000	53,000	61,000
Number of houses built	240	190	175
Number of sports centres	0	2	2
Number of entertainment complexes	2	2	3

1 Summerville had a *smaller / largest /* (*higher*) population in 2019 than 2015.
2 Average house prices were the *lowest / highest / tallest* in 2023.
3 In 2015 the population was the *higher / greatest / lowest*.
4 The number of *houses / sports centres / entertainment complexes* built was higher in 2023 than 2019.
5 The number of houses built in 2015 was *lower / higher / the largest*.

Places to live 71

Part 2: Skills development

ℹ Exam information: Comparing more than one visual

For Task 1 you may have to compare and describe two or more charts, graphs or tables. These may show information about the same topic but focus on different aspects.

You will need to understand what information each chart / graph / table shows and find any relationships between them, e.g. notice a change in one table / chart / graph that may be caused / be the cause of a change in another table / chart / graph.

1 Look at the bar chart and the two pie charts below and complete the sentences opposite.

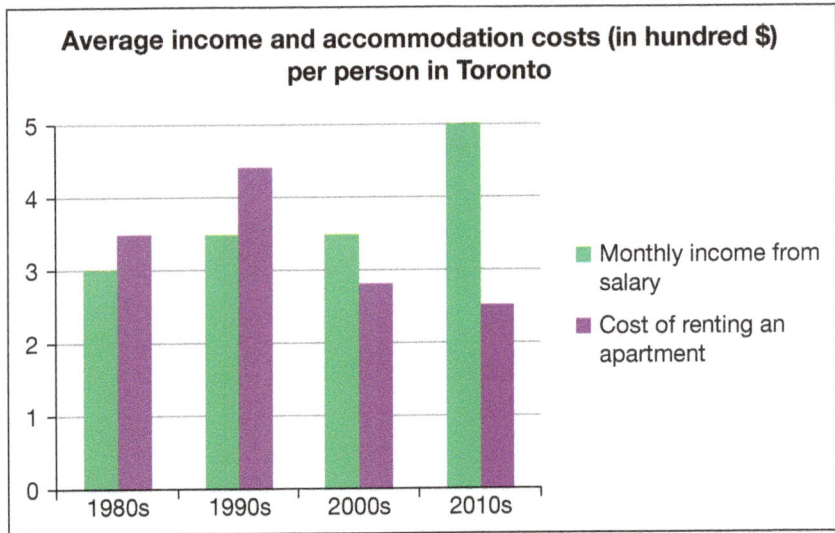

Proportion of monthly income spent on different living expenses

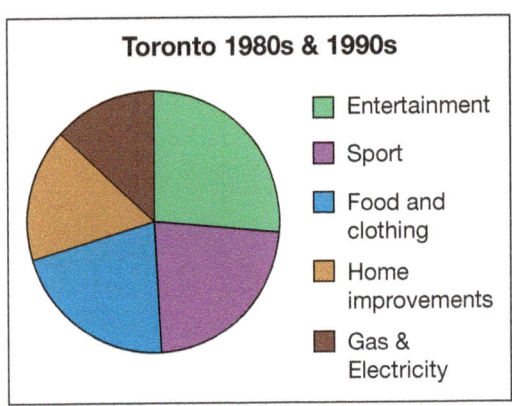 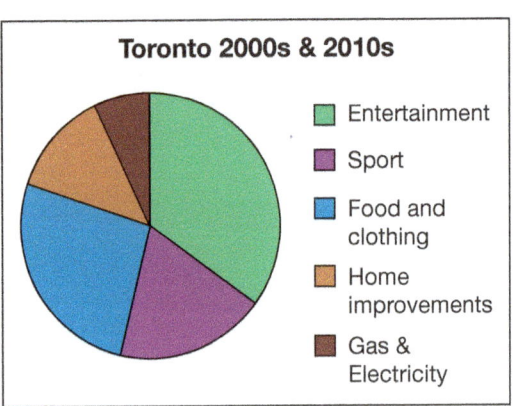

72   Writing for IELTS

Unit 10

1. During the 2000s and 2010s people in Toronto spent more on entertainment because they ___had higher salaries___.

2. Due to higher monthly salaries people spent more on food and clothing in the _____.

3. Spending on entertainment was _____ in the 1990s because the cost of renting an apartment was high.

4. People spent more on sport and entertainment in the 2000s because it was _____ to rent an apartment.

5. In the 1990s the _____ was the highest so people spent less on other things.

6. In the 2010s monthly salaries were high and rent costs were low so people spent more on _____ than in the 1990s.

> ### 💡 Exam tip: Main trends
> Remember to find the **main trends** shown by the graph(s) / chart(s). Don't describe all the details of the information shown. Look at these example sentences describing the charts in Exercise 1:
>
> *The cost of renting an apartment was low in the 2000s so people spent more on other things.* = MAIN TREND
>
> *Spending on gas and electricity in Toronto was higher in the 1980s than in the 2000s.* = DETAIL

2 Now read the following sentences and decide which are the main trends and which are details according to the charts in Exercise 1. Write M (main trends) or D (details).

1. The money spent on home improvements was less in the 2000s and 2010s. _D_
2. Spending on leisure activities grew over this period. ____
3. Monthly incomes in Toronto increased from the 1980s to 2010s. ____
4. The cost of renting an apartment has decreased since the 1980s. ____
5. People have spent more on entertainment and sport in recent years. ____
6. From the 1980s to the 1990s monthly salaries and the cost of renting an apartment increased. ____
7. In the 2010s people's spending on entertainment was higher. ____

Places to live

3 Look at the graph and the bar chart below and decide if the sentences are True or False. Write T or F.

1 Land used for housing has decreased since 1990. _T_
2 The city of Newtown has expanded the amount of its park land over the last 30 years. ____
3 The cost of all land types increased in 2020. ____
4 In 2010 more land was used for housing than for offices and shops. ____
5 The price of business land was the highest in 1990. ____
6 The amount of land used for business purposes grew from 2010 to 2020. ____

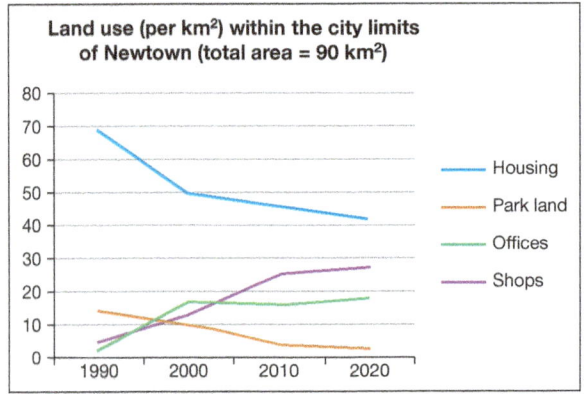

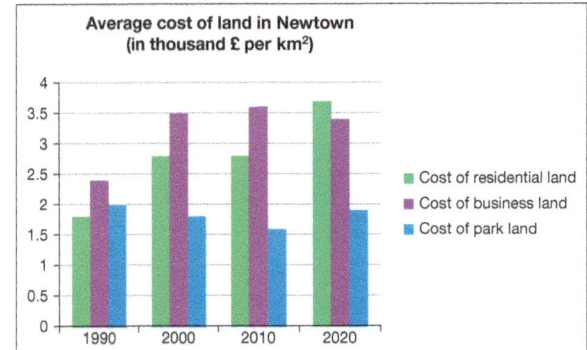

4 Expand these notes into full sentences to describe the graph and bar chart in Exercise 3.

1 cost of residential land = increase / land use for housing = decrease / since 1990
   Since 1990 the cost of residential land has increased so the land used for housing has decreased.

2 2000 to 2010 / business land cost = slight rise / land used for shops and offices = same
3 since 2010 / cost of business land and business land use = stable
4 housing land use / decrease / last 40 years / reason = cost
5 land used for offices / from 1990 to 2010 / grew
6 cheapest land = park land / 1990 – 2020

Part 3: Exam practice

Writing Task 1

You should spend about 20 minutes on this task.

The pie charts and the table show the types of living accommodation occupied by 25-year-olds in Belfast during the 2000s and the 2020s and the availability of different types of accommodation in Belfast during the same two periods.

Summarize the information by selecting and reporting the main features, and make comparisons where relevant.

Write at least 150 words.

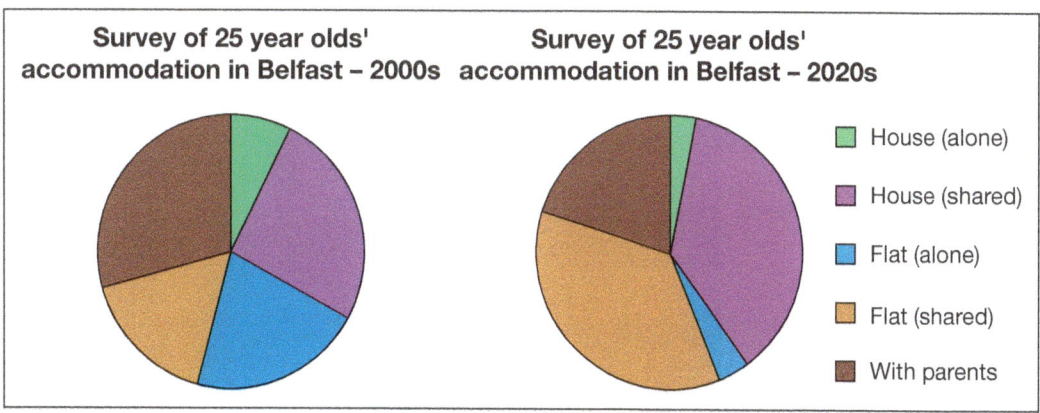

	Available housing in Belfast: 2000s and 2020 onwards			
	1–2 bedroom houses	1–2 bedroom flats	3–4 bedroom houses	3–4 bedroom flats
2000s	34,000	32,000	47,000	39,000
2020s	12,000	10,000	48,500	32,000

⇒ Progress Check

How many boxes can you tick? You should work towards being able to tick them all.

Did you...
use the present perfect to describe recent changes in the past that are still continuing, have only just finished or are having an effect now? ☐
use comparative and superlative structures to compare data? ☐
look for any links between the information which multiple charts / tables / graphs show? ☐
write about the main trends and then support these with relevant details? ☐

11 Health

Language development | Health vocabulary, First and second conditionals
Exam skills | Cause and effect, Indefinite language
Exam practice | Task 2 Cause and effect essay

Part 1: Language development

Vocabulary: Health and healthcare

1 Match the pictures to the words in the box.

a

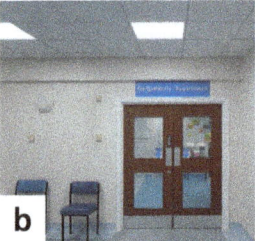
b

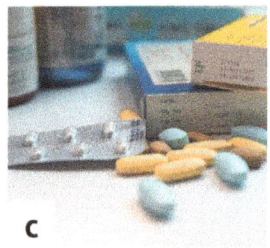
c

d

| patient | hospital | medicine | doctor |

2 Complete the texts with the words from the box.

| cure | ill | junk food | fitter | medicines |
| overweight | exercise | illness | live |

Nowadays, many children are (1) __overweight__ . There are many reasons for this; some people blame the amount of (2) _____ that is available, and others claim it is because children don't get enough (3) _____ . The reality is that childhood obesity is probably a combination of both poor diet and lack of exercise.

Doctors have been trying to find a (4) _____ for the common cold for many years. A cold, which is a relatively harmless (5) _____ , can occur at any time of the year and may mean that a person cannot work for up to a week. There are many (6) _____ for treating colds. However, they cannot cure them.

It is often claimed that exercise keeps people (7) _____ and healthier, and a recent study has shown that this is true. People who do at least 40 minutes of exercise a week, for example jogging or swimming, are less likely to become (8) _____ , and are more likely to (9) _____ to old age.

Writing for IELTS

Unit 11

Grammar: The first conditional

The first conditional is used to show causes and effects in real situations. First conditional structures have two clauses. The if-clause contains a condition or cause and the main clause contains the result or effect of the condition or cause.

if-clause (condition / cause)	main clause (result / effect)
if + present simple	+ subject + *will / should / could / might / may* + infinitive without *to*

If my cold gets worse, I will go to bed. **or** *I will go to bed if my cold gets worse.*

3 Complete the sentences with phrases a–d. Then underline all the result clauses.

1. If doctors find a cure for the common cold, _____ .
2. _____ if they eat too much junk food.
3. If people exercise every day, _____ .
4. _____ if hospitals aren't free.

a. Children might become overweight
b. people will have fewer absences from work
c. they may live longer
d. People may suffer

Grammar: The second conditional

The second conditional is used to show causes and effects in unlikely situations. Second conditional structures have two clauses. The if-clause contains a condition or cause and the main clause contains the result or effect of the condition or cause.

if-clause (condition / cause)	main clause (result / effect)
if + past simple	+ subject + *would / could / might* + infinitive without *to*

If all illnesses were cured, everybody would be happy.
or *Everybody would be happy if all illnesses were cured.*

4 Use these notes to write full sentences with the second conditional. Keep the information in the order given.

1. Doctors receive better training. Patient care improve.
   If doctors received better training, patient care would improve.
2. Junk food not exist. People not be overweight.
3. People live longer. All diseases cured.
4. Hospitals free. More people live longer.
5. No doctors. A lot more illness.

> **⚠ Watch out**
>
> Remember that there is only ONE clause with *will* / *would* in conditional sentences:
>
> If we will eat more fruit, we **will** be more healthy. ✗
>
> If we eat more fruit, we **will** be more healthy. ✓

Health 77

Part 2: Skills development

Exam information: A cause and effect essay
For Task 2 you might need to write about the causes and effects of a problem or issue. Use conditional sentences and linking words such as *because, so, therefore, as a result (of)* to describe causes and effects clearly.

1 Read the essay paragraph and underline the cause and effect sentences. Then label each cause (C) and each effect (E).

> *A country which has free healthcare has a healthier population.* To what extent do you agree or disagree?

Healthcare should be free in every country because it helps improve the health of the population. Some things such as computers, cars or holidays are luxuries which people should pay for themselves, but healthcare is a necessity not a luxury. *(C)* If people do not have access to free healthcare, *(E)* minor health problems may become much worse. Also, the cost of healthcare should not stop people from going to the doctor. If poor people have to pay for healthcare, they might not visit the doctor when they are ill. If healthcare becomes more expensive, there may be some negative effects in the future. For example, if only rich people can afford healthcare, they may be much healthier and may live longer than poor people. The result of this could be an unequal and divided society.

Exam tip: Indefinite language
Only use *will* / *would* in the result clause of a conditional sentence if you are stating a well known fact. In an essay, it is usually better to use indefinite language such as *may / can / could / might* to describe opinions or possible, rather than definite, results.

If you smoke, you will become very ill. ✗
If you smoke, you might / may become very ill. ✓

2 Complete another paragraph from the same essay using the phrases from the box.

> if people have unhealthy lifestyles   they should pay for it themselves
> free healthcare might not help them

However, free healthcare does not always result in a healthy population. For example, if people choose to have an unhealthy lifestyle, (1) _____ . Some people believe that (2) _____ , they should not receive free healthcare. In addition, healthcare comes in many forms and some of these forms of healthcare may not be essential. Most doctors think that if people want cosmetic surgery just to improve their appearance, (3) _____ . However, doctors think that the government should pay for some forms of cosmetic surgery.

Writing for IELTS

Unit 11

💡 Exam tip: Cause and effect structures

You can use other structures to describe causes and effects. Notice the order of the causes and effects and the blue words in the sentences below.

       effect   *cause*
Many people die from smoking **due to** lung damage and diseases such as cancer.

     cause   *effect*
Due to lung damage and diseases such as cancer, many people die from smoking.

      effect   *cause*
People can become fat **because** they eat too much bad food.

     cause   *effect*
Because people eat too much bad food, they can become fat.

3 Complete the sentences for the essay below using the phrases from the box, then mark each cause (C) and each effect (E).

> ***Obesity is a common problem in many societies.*** What are the main causes of obesity and what are the effects?

1 People have become accustomed to junk food *(C)*, **so** *they do not eat enough vegetables. (E)*
2 **Because** young children spend too much time watching online videos, _____
3 Many people have office jobs which do not involve any physical activity. **As a result**, they _____
4 **Because** _____, children do not know how to cook for themselves.
5 **Due to** the availability of cheap fast food, _____
6 Governments earn a lot of money from fast-food companies **because** _____

> their parents do not teach them
> ~~they do not eat enough vegetables.~~
> aren't active enough.
> people do not shop for fresh food.
> they do not get enough exercise.
> they tax them heavily.

4 Underline three mistakes with linking words in this text.

> Exercise is an important part of a healthy life. If people don't exercise, they will become unhealthy. Nowadays, many people don't get enough exercise ~~due to~~ *because* they have jobs where they sit down all day. Additionally, life is easier. In the old days, people had to wash clothes by hand or make their own bread. Result, they were more active in their lives. Also, people didn't have cars in the old days, because they had to walk everywhere. This meant that people were active in their daily life. Now, due cars and machines which make life easier, people don't do as much. As a result, they become more unfit.

Health

5 Read the essay title, then match the causes to the effects in the table. Write the headings 'Causes' and 'Effects' in the correct places.

> *Modern technology is a threat to the health of people all over the world.* What are the main effects of modern technology on our health?

1 Children spend too much time sitting playing video games.	a People can develop wrist problems or back pain.
2 Using social media is a common hobby for many people nowadays.	b They cannot hear cars coming and may get run over.
3 Ready meals are easy to buy.	c They do not move enough so they become overweight.
4 Office jobs involve too much time working with computers.	d People don't cook fresh food any more.
5 People in the street listen to music through headphones.	e Face-to-face activities such as sports are less popular.

6 Use some of the causes and effects from the table above to write a paragraph for the same essay. Write approximately 60–80 words. Start your paragraph like this:

Many health problems today may be caused by modern technology. For example, _____

💡 Exam tip: Building your argument

A good way of building your argument is to write the topic sentence of a paragraph, then add a cause and effect sentence to explain the topic sentence:

An inactive lifestyle is bad for people. If people don't exercise and move around, they may become ill.

Writing for IELTS

Part 3: Exam practice

Writing Task 2

You should spend about 40 minutes on this task.

Write about the following topic:

> *Governments should introduce healthcare which prevents illness rather than cures it. How far do you agree with this statement?*

Give reasons for your answer and include any relevant examples from your own knowledge or experience.

Write at least 250 words.

> **Progress Check**
>
> **How many boxes can you tick? You should work towards being able to tick them all.**
>
> Did you...
> - use the first conditional to describe possible causes and effects? ☐
> - use the second conditional to describe unlikely causes and effects? ☐
> - use *would*, *could*, *might* and *may* rather than will to describe possible effects / results? ☐
> - use linking words to express causes and effects? ☐

12 Transport

Language development | Transport vocabulary, Verb patterns, Articles
Exam skills | Problems and solutions, Checking your work
Exam practice | Task 2 Problem and solution essay

Part 1: Language development

Vocabulary: Transport

1   Complete the speech bubbles with the words from the box. Then match each person to the correct photo.

| abroad | commute | fare | pollution | traffic jams |
| rush hour | | service | crowded | |

1   Generally, I like driving, but in the _rush hour_____, when there is a lot of traffic, it can be really frustrating. The roads are really busy here so there are _____ all the time.

2   I work in the city and I _____ to work by underground. It's really quick and easy, but it can also be extremely _____ – I almost never get a seat!

3   I take the bus to school because the _____ is cheap and there are discounts for students. Also, the _____ is fast and reliable.

4   I often travel _____ with my work, so I spend a lot of time in airports. I like flying, but I worry about the amount of _____ that is caused by the airline industry.

Grammar: Verb patterns

Some verbs can be followed by an infinitive with to or an -ing form.

Verb + infinitive with *to*
I **expect to see** him at the airport.
Everyone **wants to travel** to other countries.
I always **choose to travel** by train.
He **decided to buy** a new car.

I **promise to visit** you next week.
He **appears to be** travel sick!
We **planned to catch** the 10.30 bus.

Verb + *-ing*
I **enjoy travelling** by train.
She **suggested driving** to the airport.

Some people cannot **resist driving** everywhere.
They **considered taking** the underground.

Writing for IELTS

Unit 12

2 Circle the correct option.

1 The government promised not *to increase* / *increasing* the price of train travel.
2 Many people enjoy *to travel* / *travelling* by plane.
3 We suggest *to find* / *finding* alternative sources of fuel.
4 People want *to travel* / *travelling* cheaply.
5 Oil companies are considering *to raise* / *raising* petrol prices.
6 The government plans *to change* / *changing* their policy on air travel.
7 We can expect *to see* / *seeing* a rise in the number of people who own cars.
8 I have decided *to commute* / *commute* to work by bus.

3 Complete the text by putting the verbs in brackets in the correct form (tense followed by *to* or *-ing*).

Many people (1) ___*enjoy driving*___ (enjoy – drive), but they should try to walk as much as possible. Although using public transport is better than driving, it still pollutes the environment. If everyone (2) _____ (decide – walk) at least twice a week, this might have a significant effect on levels of pollution. People who (3) _____ (choose – walk) to work or school might also become fitter. People who manage to walk a short distance every day (4) _____ (appear – feel) healthier and less stressed. Unfortunately many people are unable (5) _____ (resist – use) their cars because they have busy lives.

Grammar: Articles

To talk about things in general, we often use a noun with zero (= no) article or a plural:

*I try to use **public transport**. (not 'the public transport')*
***Cars** cause a lot of pollution (not 'the cars')*

However, with specific nouns we need an article (*a* / *an* or *the*):

*Get into **the car**. (= I know which car).*   *I want to buy **a car**. (= I don't know which car)*
***The sun** is a long way from **the Earth**. (= only one sun and one earth in our solar system.)*

4 Complete the sentences with the correct form of the noun in brackets (plural, zero article or plus *a* / *an* / *the*).

1 ___*Trains*___ cause less pollution than cars. (train)
2 _____ is a common problem in cities. (pollution)
3 _____ is a common way of travelling in town. (public transport)
4 _____ are one of the most popular forms of transport. (car)
5 You'll need _____ to travel to other countries. (passport)
6 You can book flights and accommodation on _____ . (internet)

Part 2: Skills development

ⓘ Exam information: A problem and solution essay

For Task 2 you might need to write a problem and solution essay. For this essay you will need to think about and explain the problems of a situation or issue and consider and evaluate more than one possible solution.

There are two possible structures for a problem and solution essay:

1   Introduce the situation in the introduction
    Paragraph 1 = problem 1 + solution(s)
    Paragraph 2 = problem 2 + solution(s)
    Conclusion

2   Introduce the situation in the introduction
    Paragraph 1 = all problems
    Paragraph 2 = all solutions
    Conclusion

1 Read the essay title and the list of problems and solutions below. Decide which are problems and which are solutions. Write P (problem) or S (solution) next to each idea.

> **Many cities suffer from traffic-related problems.** What problems does traffic cause in cities and what are the possible solutions?

1   The government should increase vehicle tax. _S_
2   People should use their cars less and public transport more. ____
3   Traffic jams create stress in people's lives. ____
4   The cost of travelling by bus or train needs to be cheaper. ____
5   There is a lot of air pollution in cities. ____
6   Public transport is too crowded. ____
7   Many accidents happen because there are so many cars on the roads. ____
8   If driving tests were more difficult, there would be fewer cars on the roads. ____

2 Look at these ideas for the essay in Exercise 1 and match problems 1–4 to solutions a–d.

	Problems		Solutions
1	Traffic jams are caused by too many cars and lorries.	a	People should pay to drive into cities during busy times such as mornings and evenings.
2	Public transport is expensive so people do not use it.	b	The government could help reduce train and bus fares.
3	Air pollution caused by traffic has increased health problems.	c	The number of vehicles allowed into city centres should be limited to reduce the amount of traffic.
4	Traffic problems in cities increase journey times to work and school.	d	Electric cars should be cheaper.

Unit 12

3 Read this essay title and expand the notes in the paragraphs below into full sentences. Then number each paragraph below in the correct order (1–4) to match structure 1 for a problem and solution essay (see the Exam information box).

> Public transport is essential but problematic. Describe some of the problems connected to public transport and suggest some solutions.

Exam tip: Decide on a structure
Decide which problem and solution essay structure you prefer before taking the IELTS exam and do not change your mind during the exam.

Paragraph A: problem 2: poor / slow service: e.g. too many stops / slow journeys, bad links between buses/trains, lack of public transport in countryside; solutions: fast lanes/routes for buses; coordinate bus/train timetables; cheaper fares for travellers in country ☐

Paragraph B: public transport essential – going to/from work, school, etc.; expensive – crowded; needs better planning, etc. Essay will describe problems / suggest possible solutions ☐

Paragraph C: problem 1: cost / high fares, people do not use public transport = more cars; solutions: reduce fares for some people, e.g. old / students; make driving and cost of cars / parking more expensive / tax more → public transport = cheaper ☐

Paragraph D: although challenges, solutions for these challenges; overall public transport is good thing; must be properly planned ☐

Transport 85

💡 Exam tip: Checking your work

It is important to check your writing for common mistakes before the end of the exam because it could improve your score. Here are some key areas where mistakes often occur:

Singular / plural: There are many **type** of transport. type ✗ types ✓
Subject / verb agreement: Train fares **costs** too much money. costs ✗ cost ✓
Incorrect part of speech: Traffic jams make people **anger**. anger ✗ angry ✓

4 Underline and correct six errors in the paragraph for this essay title.

Air travel causes a variety of problems in the world and we should find alternative means of transport. Describe some of the problems caused by air travel and suggest some solutions.

First of all, air travel is a major causes of air pollution. The number of flights have increased dramatically over the last thirty years because people travel more for business, holidays and to visit friends and family. The pollution from air travel contributes significant to climate change. To reduce the effect of air travel on the environment, governments should spend most money on scientific research. Scientists must try to find a different type of fuel which does not harming the environment as much. In addition, governments could offer tax reduce to airline companies that are more environmentally friendly.

5 Read the paragraph below and match the underlined mistakes 1–6 to the categories a–f below. Then correct the mistakes.

Secondly, air travel is too (1) <u>cheaper</u> so many people choose to fly rather than take other (2) <u>form</u> of transport. Governments should introduce new laws to increase the cost of flying. If airline companies decided (3) <u>charging</u> passengers more, people (4) <u>must</u> decide to use other forms of (5) <u>the</u> public transport such as trains or ships. Another solution could be to limit the number of flights in specific parts of the world or limit the number of flights each person (6) <u>take</u> in one year.

1	___e___	a	singular / plural	_____
2	_____	b	infinitive with *to* / *-ing* form	_____
3	_____	c	incorrect article	_____
4	_____	d	subject / verb agreement	_____
5	_____	e	incorrect word form	_____
6	_____	f	incorrect modal verb	_____

💡 Exam tip: Know your mistakes

While you prepare for the IELTS writing exam, write a list of the mistakes that you often make. In the real exam, make sure you leave enough time (e.g. 5 minutes) to check your writing for spelling and grammar mistakes.

Part 3: Exam practice

Writing Task 2

You should spend about 40 minutes on this task.

Write about the following topic:

> *Motorways, or multi-lane highways, help people travel quickly and cover long distances but they also cause problems. What are the problems of motorways and what solutions are there?*

Give reasons for your answer and include any relevant examples from your own knowledge or experience.

Write at least 250 words.

Progress Check

How many boxes can you tick? You should work towards being able to tick them all.

Did you...
- use verbs followed by an infinitive with *to* and verbs followed by an *-ing* form accurately? ☐
- use plural nouns or zero article to talk about things in general? ☐
- use the correct structure for a problem and solution essay? ☐
- check your writing for grammar and spelling errors? ☐

Review 4

1 Correct one mistake in each sentence.

1. Some big city suffer from overcrowding.
2. This is often due people coming to cities for work.
3. London has grow rapidly over the last 50 years and now has over 8 million people.
4. This means that moving around the city is difficult in rushing hour and house prices are very expensive.
5. If I was the mayor of London, I will build more flats on park land, so that more people could afford a place to live.
6. If London will grow bigger, more public transport will be needed for people who work.
7. The government needs to consider to reduce the number of cars coming into cities.
8. People may decide travelling by public transport if the system improves.
9. As the result, the roads will be clearer.
10. This would make transports in general easier.

2 Complete the crossword.

Across
2 Too many people in one place (adjective)
6 Change something totally (verb)

Down
1 Place where lots of companies have offices (noun)
2 Travel to and from work (verb)
3 To put harmful things into the environment (noun)
4 People take this when they are ill (noun)
5 Food that is unhealthy (noun)

3 Look at the pie charts and the graph and correct seven mistakes in the text below.

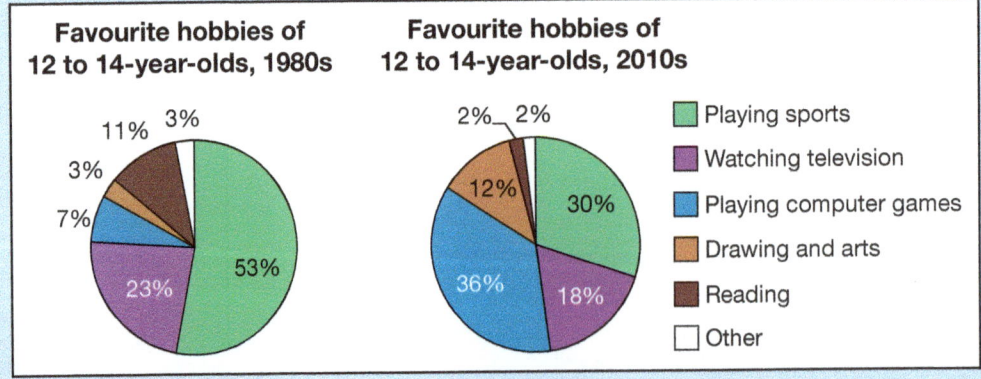

Writing for IELTS

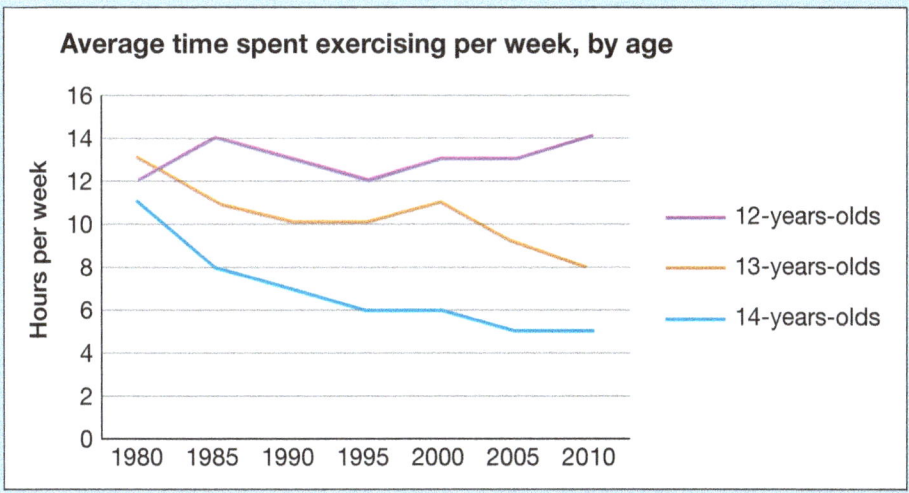

The information shows the favourite hobbies of 12 to 16-year-olds in the 1980s and 2010s and the amount of exercise they have done over this period. The information shows that favourite hobbies have changed, and also that the amount of weekly exercise has decreased for some age groups.

In the 2010s, 12 to 14-year-olds prefer activities which involve exercise. We can see that in the 1980s just over two thirds of 12 to 14 year olds named playing sports as their favourite hobby, whereas in the 2010s this number was just under a third. In the 2010s, watching TV was the most popular hobby.

This change is also reflected in the amount of exercise done by this age group. Although the amount of exercise done by 14-year-olds remained about the same throughout this period, the amount of weekly exercise done by 13 and 14-year-olds rose. In 1980, 13-year-olds did 13 hours of exercise per week on average. This decreased to 8 hours per week in 2010. This drop was steeper in 14-year-olds, from 11 hours per week in 1980 to 3 hours per week in 2010.

4 Look at the notes below on causes and effects and problems and solutions. Mark the cause / effect or problem / solution in each set of notes and expand each note into a complete sentence.

1 Pollution in cities needs to be reduced – make laws to stop car emissions and other pollutants
2 Overcrowding in cities – People moving to cities for work
3 Obesity leads to ill health – Create free exercise programmes
4 Make driving more expensive – Too many cars on the road
5 Public transport becoming more expensive – People using cars more

Practice test

Writing Task 1

You should spend about 20 minutes on this task.

The bar chart shows the types of music downloaded in the USA in 2021 by age group. Summarize the information by selecting and reporting the main features, and make comparisons where relevant.

Write at least 150 words.

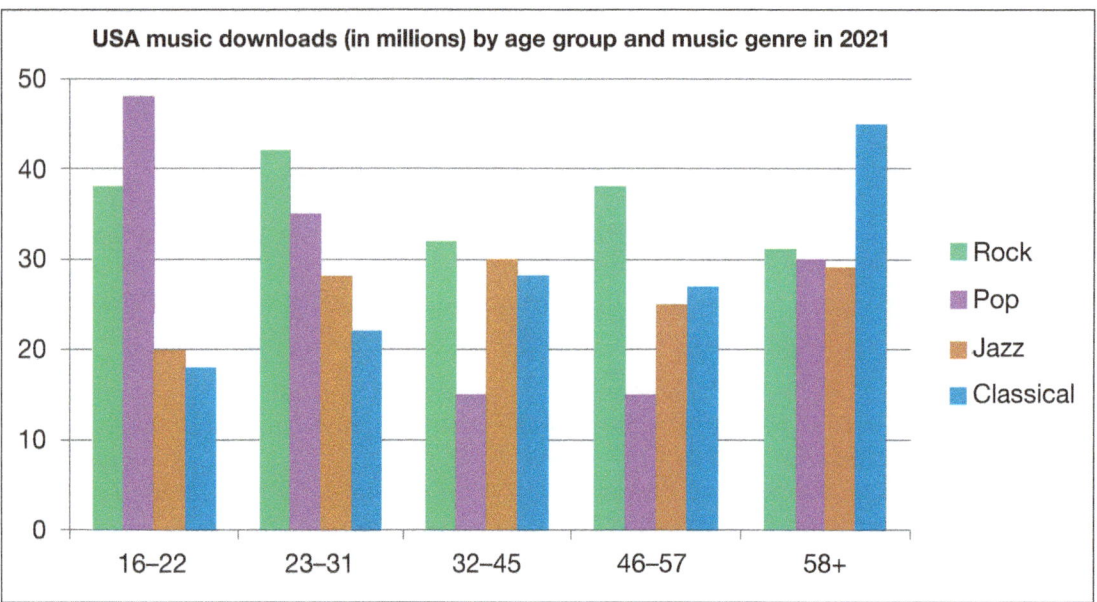

Writing Task 2

You should spend about 40 minutes on this task.

Write about the following topic:

People should choose jobs that make them happy rather than jobs with a high salary.

How far do you agree with this statement?

Give reasons for your answer and include any relevant examples from your own knowledge or experience.

Write at least 250 words.

Answer key

Unit 1 Hobbies and interests

Part 1: Language development

Exercise 1
2 watch TV
3 go swimming / swim
4 listen; music

Exercise 2

do	go	play	watch
yoga gymnastics karate	[swimming] shopping skating horse riding	the guitar computer games golf football the violin	swimming gymnastics skating golf football karate TV

Exercise 3
1 doing
2 doing
3 going
4 goes
5 go
6 playing
7 play
8 plays

Exercise 4
0 no not much/not many few some a lot of all 100
2 All
3 No
4 Some / A lot of
5 Few / Not many

Part 2: Skills development

Exercise 1
2 hockey
3 Football
4 tennis
5 cricket

Exercise 2

1 F This is false because the number of hours is small (1.5)
2 F This is false because the table shows the number of hours teenagers spend on the activities NOT the number of teenagers that like the activities.
3 T This is true because the table shows the number of hours each group spends on each activity.
4 T This is true because the numbers in the table show a low number of hours.
5 F This is false because the number of hours is 3 which is low.

Exercise 3
b best explains the table because it includes all the information and uses different words.
a does not include enough information.
c copies the title using the same words so it is not as good as (b).

Exercise 4
1 See the circled verbs in the introductions below. The verbs are in the present simple.
2 A's first sentence explains the title of the table accurately because the table shows how much time people spend on the internet. B's first sentence is inaccurate because the table does not show how much people like the internet.
3 See the underlined details in the introductions below.
4 Introduction A is better because it explains the table correctly and contains general information. Introduction B does not explain the table correctly and contains too many details.

Introduction A: The table (shows) how much time the age groups (spend) on different types of online activity. There (are) six age ranges in the table from 10–15 to over 50. The online activities in(clude) shopping, social media and playing games.

Introduction B: The table (shows) how much people (like) the internet depending on their age. 70% of children between ages 10–15 (play) games online and no children between ages 10–15 (like) shopping. Most older people (read) news sites. They (spend) 54% of their time reading the news online.

Exercise 5
1 younger age groups
2 much
3 16–20
4 10–15
5 No
6 older
7 like
8 shopping

Part 3: Exam practice

Task 1: Model answer

The table shows the number of people in millions who watch sports on television. It shows the number of viewers for four sports in four different countries.

The table shows that more American people watch sport on television than the other three nationalities. In all four countries tennis is the most popular sport on television. The total number of viewers for tennis is nearly 26 million and in each country about 6–7 million people watch it.

Not many people like watching motor racing on television compared to the other sports. In the USA and Canada only 1–1.5 million people watch motor racing but it is more popular in the UK and Australia. Golf is very popular in the USA with 11 million viewers but it is not as popular in the other countries.

Unit 2   Education

Part 1:   Language development

Exercise 1
2 teacher
3 exam
4 lectures
5 presentation

Exercise 2

verbs	nouns
[take] / sit / do / pass / fail	an exam
get	a qualification
take / do / study / pass / fail	a course
do / write	an essay
take / do / study / pass / fail	a subject
do / give / make	a presentation

Exercise 3
2 study / do
3 take / sit / do / pass
4 write / do
5 give / make / do
6 sit / take / do / pass
7 get

Exercise 4
2 One; started
3 Five; eight; started
4 Thirty-four; continued
5 thirteen; didn't go
6 Eight; decided

Exercise 5
2 Bilsing School had as many boys as girls / as many girls as boys.
3 Roysters School had fewer boys than girls / had more girls than boys.
4 Bilsing School had fewer students than Roysters School.
5 Roysters School had more students than Bilsing School.

Part 2:   Skills development

Exercise 1
1 The numbers of students
2 According to school, and then divided into boys and girls
3 Boys and girls
4 2021

Exercise 2
2 40 thousand
3 20 thousand
4 English
5 History
6 more
7 Geography
8 Art

Exercise 3

Model answer
However, there were bigger differences in the numbers of boys achieving pass grades across the subjects. The number of boys with pass grades ranged from the highest number of just over 70 thousand to the lowest number of just under 30 thousand, a difference of around 50 thousand. Boys did best in Maths, English and Science. Boys had the highest pass rate in any subject: just over 70 thousand in Maths. Their lowest pass rate was in Geography. Boys achieved more passes than girls in two subjects: Maths and Science.

Part 3   Exam Practice

Task 1: Model answer
The bar chart shows the numbers (in thousands) of students who chose to study different university subjects in 2005. The numbers for each subject are divided into male and female students and show some general differences between men's and women's choice of subjects.

Science and Maths were the most popular choices for male students in 2005, but non-science subjects were more popular with female students. The most popular subjects for female students were less technical subjects such as social sciences, languages, literature and humanities. Social sciences was by far the most popular subject for women. However, very few female students chose to study mathematics and law: four and six thousand students respectively. Almost no men – only two thousand – chose to study languages and very few men chose the arts. However, just as many men as women chose to study humanities.

Unit 3 Culture

Part 1: Language development

Exercise 1
Photo a: architecture
Photo b: a museum
Photo c: a concert
Photo d: an art gallery

2 A concert
3 Architecture
4 An art gallery

Exercise 2
useful P
interesting P
tiring N
creative P
amazing P
beautiful P
harmless P
terrible N

Exercise 3
A 2 beautiful 3 tiring
B 1 interesting 2 dangerous 3 harmless 4 terrible

Exercise 4
2 Louise gave me a bestselling book for my birthday.
3 My sister and I saw a Shakespeare play in London.
4 Tokyo has many interesting art galleries nowadays.
5 Older people like opera more than young people.
6 Most teenagers listen to music online.

Exercise 5
1 Maria likes reading detective novels and books about history.
2 My parents go to the cinema at weekends but they do not watch television.
3 Young people should watch less television because most programmes are not educational. (because)
4 The Science Museum is free so I think it is good for families.

Part 2: Skills development

Exercise 1
c Free entrance to museums and art galleries

2 How much do you agree that it is a good idea for museums and art galleries to be free for cultural reasons?

Exercise 2
a How much do you agree that if children watch too much television they do not learn or develop well?

Exercise 3
1 D
2 A
3 A
4 D

Exercise 4
2 Q
3 Q
4 T
5 Q
6 Q

Exercise 5
Suggested answers:
2 Modern culture is important because *it helps us understand the world today*.
3 Young people prefer modern culture but *it is not always better than traditional culture*.
4 Both traditional and modern culture are popular so *we should encourage both of them*.

Preserving traditional culture helps people understand the past and that will help them in the future.

Young people are more interested in modern culture so traditional culture is likely to disappear naturally.

Traditional culture may not be relevant to modern life so it is not as important.

Modern culture may come from a foreign country and bring strange values and customs.

Modern culture focuses more on the present and the future so people forget about traditional ways.

Traditional culture is often more important for older people but it should be preserved.

Part 3: Exam practice

Task 2: Model answer

Some people think that young people should spend their free time on cultural activities like music, film and theatre. Others believe that playing sport is better for young people. In my opinion, both culture and sports are important parts of life so young people should do a mixture of both.

Sport gives young people the chance to exercise, which is important for health reasons. Sport also teaches young people about rules and teamwork. Cultural activities are good for the health of the mind and spirit and allow young people to be creative and experience different worlds. However going to the theatre or learning a musical instrument can be expensive. Sports activities can be less expensive but can be dangerous and lead to injury.

In my opinion, doing only one type of activity – just sport or just music, for example – can be bad. Many young people concentrate on one activity in order to become the best, like young sports stars. This can put a lot of pressure on them and make them less interesting than someone who does a variety of things.

I believe that young people should have the chance to do a variety of activities and that a balance of sport and cultural activities is best.

Review 1

Exercise 1
1. but
2. improved
3. do
4. because
5. play
6. Many
7. many
8. as

Exercise 2
~~All~~ *Some* people think museums are more important than sport but other people do not agree. In my opinion, art is much more important than sport.

Firstly, art shows the *culture of a country* ~~of a country the culture~~ so the government should give money to museums and galleries. If we did not have museums, we would not have *much / a lot of* ~~many~~ culture in the world. However, it is expensive to run a museum or art gallery *so* ~~because~~ the government should help pay for this.

Sport is important too because it is fun and *exciting / interesting* ~~boring~~ but people do not need *much / a lot of* ~~many~~ money to enjoy it. People *play* ~~playing~~ sport in the park or they like *watching* ~~watch~~ it on television. These activities are cheap and they do not need money from the government.

Exercise 3
1. The graph shows how much money Cedar Trees School spent on different facilities from 2000 to 2010.
2. We can see that in general the school spent most money on technology.
3. From 2000 to 2010 the school increased the money spent on technology from $3,000 to $3,500.
4. Also, the money for buildings rose from $2,000 to $3,000.
5. However, not as much money was spent on sport in 2010; the money for sport went down from $2,000 to about $1,500.

Exercise 4
1. A
2. D
3. D
4. A
5. D

Unit 4 Family

Part 1: Language development

Exercise 1
2 son
3 daughter
4 father
5 grandmother
6 mother-in-law
7 grandson
8 parents

Exercise 2
2 must
3 should
4 shouldn't
5 don't need to
6 might

Exercise 3
2 I *will* go to university in the future.
3 Children *shouldn't* eat fast food.
4 Computers *might / could* do most jobs in the future.
5 Children *must / have to / need to* be taught basic skills like maths and reading.

Exercise 4
1 Children who don't *study might / could fail* their exams.
2 University *should* prepare people for the best jobs.
3 Children *should* follow their parents' advice.

Part 2: Skills development

Exercise 1
1 F   3 T   5 F
2 T   4 F   6 T

Exercise 2
Paragraph A follows the rules in Exercise 1.

Paragraph B uses definite language, e.g. *children will be really terrible, rules must be taught*. The sentence containing the main idea is at the end of the paragraph. Paragraph C contains more than one main idea (rules, beliefs and social skills) and the ideas supporting the main idea aren't clear.

Exercise 3
Suggested answers:
2 Families should do things together.
3 It is important for children to grow up with brothers and sisters. / Parents should have more than one child.
4 Children should not help with housework.

Exercise 4
Paragraph 1: c
Paragraph 2: d
Paragraph 3: b
Paragraph 4: a

Exercise 5
1 Introduction = a
2 Main body = c
3 Conclusion = b

Part 3: Exam practice

Task 2: Model answer
Some people say that children should always follow their parents' advice; others claim that this is not always right. I believe that children should follow their parents' advice when they are young, but they should become more independent when they are older.

Young children do not know the difference between right and wrong, and a parent is the best person to teach them this. For example, a young child does not know that it is wrong to take things that do not belong to them. Parents can also teach children about dangers, both in the home and outside.

However, when children grow older they should pay less attention to their parents. This is because parents might tell a child which career to choose, and this should be the child's decision. Parents sometimes want to tell their children how to live, but when they are grown up, they can decide for themselves. If a child doesn't make their own decisions, he or she might grow up to be less independent and strong.

In conclusion, parents need to give young children advice on morals and safety, but not on how to live when they are older.

Unit 5 Tourism

Part 1: Language development

Exercise 1
1 [to increase], to rise, to go up
2 to fall, to decrease, to go down, to drop
3 to remain stable, to stay the same
4 to fluctuate

Exercise 2
1 an increase
2 rose
3 decreased
4 a fall
5 went down
6 a drop
7 fluctuated

Exercise 3
1 rapid increase / sharp rise / rapid rise
2 fluctuated
3 sharp drop / sharp fall / sharp decrease / rapid drop / rapid fall / rapid decrease
4 rose sharply / rose rapidly / increased sharply / increased rapidly

Exercise 4
1 between / and
2 for
3 between / in
4 from

Part 2: Skills development

Exercise 1
2 T
3 F
4 F
5 T
6 F

Exercise 2
1 shows
2 dropped
3 went down
4 will stay the same

Exercise 3
1 shows
2 visited
3 went
4 between
5 fluctuated
6 travelled
7 dropped
8 rose
9 in
10 see
11 was
12 remained stable
13 increased

Part 3: Exam practice

Task 1: Model answer

The line graph shows the percentage of tourists to Scotland who visited certain Edinburgh attractions between 1993 and 2023. We can see that in 1993 and in 2023 the favourite attractions were the castle and the festival. In 1993 the least popular attraction was the zoo but in 2023 this changed and the aquarium was the least popular.

During the 1990s and 2000s there was a rapid increase in visitors to the castle from 25% to 45% and then the percentage gradually went down to 30% in 2023. The trend for the aquarium was similar to the castle. Visitors increased rapidly from 20% to 35% from 1993 to 1998 then gradually decreased to less than 10% over the next twenty-five years. The number of tourists who visited the festival fluctuated slightly but in general remained stable at about 25%. Visitors to the zoo also fluctuated from 1998 to 2013 then rose sharply from 10% to 20% between 2013 and 2023.

Unit 6 Films

Part 1: Language development

Exercise 1
2 Action
3 Documentary
4 Thriller
5 Horror Film
6 Science Fiction

Exercise 2
2 soundtrack
3 story
4 effects
5 genres
6 blockbusters

Exercise 3
1 documentary; story
2 science fiction; special effects
3 genre; soundtracks; horror

Exercise 4
25 per cent = a quarter
75 per cent = three quarters
33 per cent = a third
66 per cent = two thirds

Exercise 5
1 A third of adults do not watch science fiction films.
2 Ten per cent of worldwide film sales come from Bollywood.
3 Three quarters of people over 65 watch films on television.
4 Ninety per cent of children watch cartoons on a regular basis.

Exercise 6
1 c
2 d
3 b
4 a

Part 2: Skills development

Exercise 1
2 A
3 B
4 A
5 B
6 A

Exercise 2
Suggested answers:
Just over a third of cinema visitors are between 25 and 39.
Almost 25 percent of cinema visitors are young people aged 13 to 24 years old.
Just under a quarter of people who visit the cinema are between 13 and 24 years old.
Nearly a third of people who visit the cinema are over 55 years old.

Exercise 3
2 T
3 F
4 T
5 T
6 F
7 T
8 T
9 F
10 T

Exercise 4
2 story
3 publicity
4 a quarter / 25 per cent
5 about / approximately
6 Two thirds / 66 per cent
7 five per cent
8 proportion / number / percentage
9 approximately / about
10 per cent

Part 3: Exam Practice

Task 1: Model answer

The pie charts show the proportions of Oscar winners for seven different genres of film in 2013 and 2023. Between 2013 and 2023 the proportion of films that won Oscars changed for nearly all the genres. In particular, many more action films and science fiction films gained Oscars in 2013 than in 2023.

The proportion of thrillers that won Oscars went down from about half of the total in 2013 to a third in 2023. The number of horror films that won Oscars also decreased by about half from 2013 to 2023. Action, documentary and science fiction films all increased their share of Oscars between 2013 and 2023. Action films increased from about 20 per cent of the total in 2013 to almost a quarter in 2023. The proportion of Oscar winners for documentaries, romance and science fiction all increased by approximately fifty percent between 2013 and 2023. The percentage for comedy films which won Oscars stayed the same in 2013 and 2023 at about 5 per cent.

Review 2

Exercise 1
1 A *horror film* is a film that scares people.
2 The number of radio listeners is increasing *slowly*.
3 Children *shouldn't* ~~to~~ be rude to older people.
4 Seventy-five per cent of people is *three quarters*.
5 You *mustn't* break laws.
6 There was a *sharp drop* in the number of people buying CDs.

Exercise 2
Paragraph 1: B; Sentence c added

Tourism has increased dramatically over the last thirty years because of easier and cheaper air travel, meaning more and more people can get to other places quickly and easily. Many people see tourism as a good thing for countries, but tourism also has many negative aspects. *I believe tourism is just as negative as it is positive because tourism can damage local culture and be bad for the environment.*

Paragraph 2: D; Sentence b added

Firstly, when an area becomes a tourist destination, it can lose some of its traditional ways. For example, tourists come and often signs are put up in foreign languages. In many tourist resorts there are bars, shops and staff that do not represent the local culture. Sometimes, a person can go on holiday and not hear the local language at all. It is important to preserve local languages and customs or they may be lost.

Paragraph 3: A; Sentence d added

Tourism is also bad for the environment in general. Busy tourist resorts can get a lot of litter, and a place that was once beautiful can become quite ugly because of this. On a larger scale, travelling long distances by air can be damaging for the planet because it creates a lot of pollution.

Paragraph 4: C; Sentence a added

These are the main reasons why tourism can be just as negative as positive. People need to think about the environment and local culture before they travel abroad on holiday. If these things aren't considered, some areas could be badly affected.

Exercise 3
The line graph shows how people liked to watch films between 1985 and 2005. We can see that some methods of watching films became less popular, while some other new methods became very popular. We can also see that watching films on TV has always stayed popular.

Firstly, both video and cinema (vi) *decreased steadily over the twenty year period*. Video watching (ii) *dropped from nearly 80% in 1985 to around 20% in 2005*. This is similar to watching films at cinemas, which (v) *fell steadily by about 20% over this time*.

Some methods of watching films have become more popular. Watching films on the internet and DVD both (iii) *increased from 1990 to 2005*. There was a (vii) *sharp rise* (from 0% to 65%) in DVD watching. Watching films on the internet (i) *rose steadily from 0%* to just under 40%. The high percentage of people who watched films on TV (iv) *remained stable* at around 80%.

Exercise 4
1 T
2 F
3 T
4 T
5 T
6 F

Unit 7 Technology

Part 1: Language development

Exercise 1
2 b
3 f
4 a
5 e
6 c

Exercise 2
Suggested answers:
1 In addition, playing video games can mean that children do less exercise.
2 Furthermore, it enables people to work more quickly.
3 Also, social media can occasionally be dangerous.

Exercise 3
Suggested answers:
1 yet playing video games can also improve children's reactions.
2 However, technology at work can also mean that people spend too much time online or chatting online with friends.
3 On the other hand, social media can make it easier to stay in touch with friends.

Exercise 4
1 Technology is a good thing because it helps people communicate more easily ~~also~~. *Also* it helps people do their jobs more efficiently.
2 People should always pay for music and not download it illegally. Downloading illegally is bad for the music industry. In addition, *it is bad for* musicians.
3 Computers have some negative points. It is not always easy to fix a computer if it goes wrong. ~~Additionally~~ *However / On the other hand*, there are lots of people who can fix computers.
4 Smartphones can be dangerous if they are used in a car. ~~However~~ *In addition / Also / Furthermore / Moreover*, they can be dangerous for pedestrians who use them when crossing the road.

Part 2: Skills development

Exercise 1
2 D
3 D
4 D
5 A
6 D
7 A
8 A

Exercise 2
1 e
2 a
3 f
4 b
5 d
6 c
7 h
8 g

Exercise 3
2 c
3 f
4 a
5 b
6 d

Exercise 4
Best sentence order: e, a, b, c, d, f

Exercise 5
Advantages: 2, 3, 5, 7
Disadvantages: 1, 4, 6, 8

Exercise 6

Model answer
There are many advantages of social media. Firstly, social media means that people can keep in touch with their friends and family easily. For example, if a person has relatives in another country, they can keep in contact using Facebook. In addition, social media helps people pass on news. Often when a news story breaks, social media help us hear the experiences and opinions of the people where the news is happening.

However, social media also has some disadvantages. Social media can be addictive, especially in young people. Young people may spend too much time on social media compared to other activities. Furthermore, nobody knows the true identity of some of the people using social media. Sometimes people think they are talking online to someone friendly, but it might be a dangerous stranger.

Exercise 7
Suggested answers:

1 Advantages: learn about other places / people / new subjects; relaxing; entertaining; cheap

   Disadvantages: poor quality programmes; inactive; addictive; watching too much is bad for health

2 Advantages: saves time; better for communication; exciting; information easier to obtain

   Disadvantages: people spend too much time using it; addictive; high cost; technological problems

3 Advantages: young people can learn to use it more quickly; good for both young and old for information and relaxation; old people can learn new skills; good for communication for old people

   Disadvantages: lots of websites unsuitable for young people; too difficult for old people to learn how to use; isolated old people prefer being with real people to sitting at a screen

Exercise 8

Model answer
On the other hand, these platforms can also have advantages in the workplace. Social media isn't limited to entertainment platforms like Facebook or TikTok. There are also work-based social media platforms which can be beneficial to companies. For example, LinkedIn lets professional people link up with other businesspeople and develop their work contacts. This may bring benefits to a business. In addition, social networking can make people happier at work. Without access to things like Facebook or TikTok, experienced staff might become unhappy in their jobs and decide to leave.

Part 3:   Exam practice

Task 2: Model answer
In the last few decades there has been a large change from shopping in stores to shopping online. This has both advantages and disadvantages but, overall, I believe the advantages are stronger than the disadvantages.

Firstly, buying products online is much easier than going to shops. It can be difficult to know where to buy some items, or perhaps these aren't available in nearby places. However, if people shop online, the choice is much wider, and the delivery is also very quick. For example, shopping online for items such as trainers gives you more options than most sports shops. Some people also prefer online shopping because they can compare products. Most shopping sites have detailed information about the products which is difficult to find in a shop. In addition, shopping online saves a lot of time. With just a few clicks, the item will be delivered to your home.

On the other hand, people claim shopping online has disadvantages. Some people say that it makes people lazy as they stay on their screens instead of going out to the shops. Furthermore, people might spend more money online. This is because they have so much choice and it is so easy to do. Finally, shopping for clothes online is not always convenient. Sometimes the clothes don't fit and need to be returned, and this can take up a lot of time.

In conclusion, although it has advantages and disadvantages, shopping online has made life so much easier in so many ways and gives shoppers much more choice.

Unit 8 Happiness

Part 1: Language development

Exercise 1
Nouns: wealth, possessions, salary, tax, poverty, savings, income

Verbs: spend, save, inherit, tax

Adjectives: [rich], wealthy

2 savings
3 salary
4 poverty
5 wealthy
6 income
7 possessions

Exercise 2
1 tax
2 salary
3 save
4 wealthy
5 spend
6 income

Exercise 3 and 4
(Underlined nouns/ideas referred to in brackets)
2 it; it (Happiness)
3 they (people)
4 It (Good weather)
5 They (Children)
6 This; they (People who inherit a lot from their parents can become wealthy overnight [x2])

Exercise 5 and 6
These changes; have P
This approach; is S
These actions; help P
This problem; is S

Part 2: Skills development

Exercise 1 and 2
1 According to the government, traditional families are the happiest. OPO
2 There are many things that can make people happy. In my view, family and friends are the most important. WO
3 Some teachers believe that children should learn how to manage money at school. They suggest that this could help the economy in the future. OPO
4 I believe that the government should provide more financial help to poor families. WO
5 My personal opinion is that having an enjoyable job is essential for happiness. WO
6 Many people argue that all citizens should pay as little tax as possible. OPO
7 I think that wealthy people should pay more tax. WO
8 Parents often claim that they need more money. OPO

Exercise 3 and 4
Money is important in life but it does not always bring happiness. Some people say that having more money makes life less stressful, while other people argue that happiness can be found in other aspects of life such as work, family or hobbies. In my view, having more money does not make people happier but it makes life easier. There are two reasons for my opinion.

1 that having more money makes life less stressful
2 that happiness can be found in other aspects of life such as work, family or hobbies
3 that having more money does not make people happier but it makes life easier
4 two reasons

Exercise 5

Model answer
Personal happiness can come from many different aspects of life. For some people happiness comes from being successful, either at work or at school or within a community. On the other hand, some people argue that personal happiness depends on being able to enjoy life and on having a positive attitude when bad things happen. I believe that personal happiness is more about individual personality and less about particular life events, personal success or possessions.

Exercise 6 and 7

1 Also / In addition / Similarly
2 although
3 However / On the other hand
4 Also / In addition
5 However / On the other hand

> **Model answer**
> Secondly, having more money can help people plan for the future so they have more control over their lives. I believe that saving money helps people to become more independent because they will not have to ask for financial help when they are old. In addition, they can plan for things like their children's education or buying a bigger house. However, people with little money cannot plan for the future easily because they have to focus on the present. Some people argue that having less money does not prevent people planning for the future, but, in my view, it makes it much more difficult.

Exercise 8 and 9

1 this
2 They
3 also
4 However / On the other hand
5 this / it
6 These
7 These
8 but / although

> **Model answer**
> Enjoying the little things in life can be another important factor in happiness. Some people think that life is about achieving great things like having a successful job and a big house, but life is also about small pleasures like having a good dinner or a nice walk in the countryside. If people enjoyed these little things more, then they might be happier in general.

Part 3: Exam Practice

Task 2: Model answer

Everybody wants to be happy, but there is often a debate over what makes a person happy. Some people believe happiness can only come from friends and family. According to other people, happiness comes from money and possessions. I believe that happiness comes both from close family and friends and also from having enough money and possessions.

Firstly, everybody needs enough money to live – to pay for a home, food and other necessities. If people have money to spare after paying for these things, they often spend money on possessions which make them feel happy for a short time. However, this kind of happiness often does not last because money and possessions alone cannot bring happiness. Rich people can be very lonely if they don't share their money and possessions with others. It has also been proved that having a good time with friends and family brings people more happiness than a fast car or new clothes.

On the other hand, very poor people are not usually happy, even if they have large families and many friends. Money worries will cause them a lot of stress and this will mean they are not able to enjoy life. Their friends and family may be able to support them and help them by lending them money, but this may lead to problems. I agree that family and friends are important, but without a good income, they may not be enough.

In conclusion, I believe that both money and possessions as well as a family and friends are important to happiness and that neither is more important than the other. People who don't have enough money to live but who have good friends and a strong family may be just as unhappy as wealthy people who have more than enough but no family or friends to share it with.

Unit 9 The natural world

Part 1: Language development

Exercise 1
1 E
2 F
3 B
4 C
5 A
6 D

Exercise 2
1 temperature
2 pollution
3 volcano

Exercise 3
2 plants are watered
3 plants grow
4 plants flower
5 flowers are picked
6 plants die

Exercise 4
2 is eaten; are eaten
3 are destroyed
4 are inhabited
5 are damaged
6 is caused

Exercise 5
2 Chemicals are used *by* farmers to protect plants from insects.
3 Seeds are *planted* in the spring.
4 Elephants and camels *are* used as working animals in some countries.
5 Volcanoes and other natural disasters is *are* studied by scientists.
6 Fields be *are* watered by a special system called irrigation.

Part 2: Skills development

Exercise 1
d – 1, e – 2, b – 3, g – 4, f – 5, h – 6, a – 7, c – 8

Exercise 2
Suggested answers:
2 Magma erupts from the crater at the top of the volcano.
3 The magma is changed / changes into lava.
4 An ash cloud forms above the volcano. / An ash cloud is formed above the volcano.
5 Lava flows down the side of the volcano.
6 Many trees are killed by lava.

Exercise 3
1 Firstly / First / First of all
2 When / After
3 then

Suggested answers:

Rocks underneath the glacier are picked up and carried along. When the glacier reaches the bottom of the mountain, it starts to melt. The ice from the glacier is turned into meltwater. Next, this meltwater becomes a river and the rocks from the glacier are deposited on the riverbed. Finally, the river flows to the sea.

Part 3: Exam Practice

Task 1: Model answer
The diagrams show the process of growing, collecting and processing wheat plants. It shows all the stages from planting the seeds to finally turning the wheat into flour.

First of all, wheat seeds are planted in the fields by farmers. It takes between four and eight months for these plants to grow enough to be harvested. When they are ready, the plants are then cut by a machine called a combine harvester.

The plants contain both wheat and straw, and a machine then separates the wheat from the straw. At this point, different things happen. The wheat is taken to a barn where it is stored, but the straw is put into bales and left in the fields. After storage, the wheat is then transported from the storage barns to factories in large trucks. Finally, the wheat is processed into flour, which can be used in everyday cooking and baking.

150 words

Review 3

Exercise 1
1 wealthy
2 Poor
3 volcano
4 savings
5 download
6 Social
7 atmosphere
8 radiation

Exercise 2
1 they
2 It / This
3 These
4 it
5 these
6 They

Exercise 3
1 New ways of communicating are created by social networking sites.
2 Animals are kept in fields (by farmers) during the day.
3 People's personal information is protected by internet companies.
4 Volcanos are caused by movement in the Earth's surface.
5 A person's level of happiness is affected by money, friends and family.
6 People all over the world are connected by social networks.

Exercise 4
The correct order is: **1:** c, **2:** f, **3:** b, **4:** d, **5:** e, **6:** g, **7:** a

Exercise 5

Model answer
Some people think that money has a negative effect on society and cannot make people happy *but others believe* that *it* has a positive effect on *them*. *I think* that money has positive and negative effects on happiness for the following reasons.

First of all, if we do not have money, life is difficult. *However*, if we have enough money, life is easier. *Some people say that / I think that* wealthy people worry less *and that* poor people worry more. *In addition*, other things in life can make people happy, *for example*, hobbies and sports. When you have hobbies and do sports, you meet people and enjoy life and *this* can be better than having lots of money.

Exercise 6
1: b A butterfly starts life as a small round egg. This egg *is laid* on the leaves of plants.

2: d When the egg hatches, a caterpillar *emerges*. The caterpillar has to eat as much as possible in order to grow.

3: a When it is the right size, the caterpillar grows a hard skin called a pupa. Inside the pupa the caterpillar *loses* its old body parts and grows completely new ones, including wings.

4: c Finally, the butterfly *is released*. After some time, it will fly away to begin its adult life and start the cycle again.

Unit 10   Places to live

Part 1:   Language development

Exercise 1
2 sports centre
3 shopping centre
4 entertainment complex
5 business park
6 industrial area

Exercise 2
2 d
3 b
4 e
5 f
6 a

Exercise 3
2 have transformed
3 has converted
4 has improved
5 has expanded
6 have reduced

Exercise 4
2 highest
3 the lowest
4 entertainment complexes
5 the largest

Part 2:   Skills development

Exercise 1
2 2000s and 2010s
3 lower
4 cheaper / less expensive
5 cost of renting an apartment
6 entertainment and food and clothing

Exercise 2
2 M
3 M
4 M
5 D
6 D
7 D

Exercise 3
2 F
3 F
4 T
5 F
6 F

Exercise 4
Suggested answers:
2 From 1990 to 2000 the cost of business land only rose slightly so the land used for shops and offices in Newtown remained the same.
3 Since 2000 the cost of business land and the amount of land used for business have remained stable.
4 The amount of land used for housing in Newtown has decreased over the last 40 years due to the increase in the cost of residential land.
5 The amount of land used for offices in Newtown grew from 1980 to 2000.
6 Between 1980 and 2010 the cheapest type of land in Newtown was park land.

Part 3:   Exam practice

Task 1: Model answer
The pie charts and table show 25-year-olds' accommodation and the availability of different types of housing in Belfast in the 2000s and 2020s. Since 2020 the lower number of available 1–2 bedroom houses and flats has reduced the housing choices for this age group.

Shared accommodation has become the most common form of housing for this age group in the 2020s. In the 2000s, only around 50% of those surveyed lived in shared houses or flats. In the 2020s this number has grown to around 75% of 25-year-olds living in Belfast. The higher number could be due to the stable availability of larger houses and flats during this period.

There was also a drop in the number of people living alone. In the 2000s around a quarter of 25-year-olds lived alone in Belfast. However, from 2020 onwards, the reduction in the availability of 1–2 bedroom houses and flats has altered this figure. In the 2000s there were 34,000 1–2 bedroom houses and 32,000 1–2 bedroom flats available. These figures dropped to 12,000 and 10,000 from 2020 onwards.

Finally, living with parents has become less common. There was a reduction in the number of 25-year-olds living with parents from around a third in the 2000s to under a quarter in 2020.

Unit 11 Health

Part 1: Language development

Exercise 1
a doctor
b hospital
c medicine
d patient

Exercise 2
2 junk food
3 exercise
4 cure
5 illness
6 medicines
7 fitter
8 ill
9 live

Exercise 3
1 b; people will have fewer absences from work
2 a; children might become overweight
3 c; they may live longer
4 d; people may suffer

Exercise 4
2 If junk food didn't exist, people would not be overweight.
3 People would live longer, if all diseases were cured.
4 If hospitals were free, more people would live longer.
5 If there were no doctors, there would be a lot more illness.

Part 2: Skills development

Exercise 1
Healthcare should be free in every country because it helps improve the health of the population. Some things such computers, cars or holidays are luxuries which people should pay for, but healthcare is a necessity not a luxury. (C) If people do not have access to free healthcare, (E) minor health problems may become much worse. Also, the cost of healthcare should not stop people from going to the doctor. (C) If poor people have to pay for healthcare, (E) they might not visit the doctor when they are ill. (C) If healthcare becomes more expensive, (E) there may be some negative effects in the future. For example, (C) if only rich people can afford healthcare, (E) they may be much healthier and may live longer than poor people. The result of this could be an unequal and divided society.

Exercise 2
1 free healthcare might not help them
2 if people have unhealthy lifestyles
3 they should pay for it themselves

Exercise 3
2 **Because** young children spend too much time watching television (C), they do not get enough exercise. (E)
3 Many people have office jobs which do not involve any physical activity (C). **As a result**, they aren't active enough (E).
4 **Because** their parents do not teach them (C), children do not know how to cook for themselves. (E)
5 **Due** to the availability of cheap fast food (C), people do not shop for fresh food (E).
6 Governments earn a lot of money from fast food companies (E) **because** they tax them heavily. (C)

Exercise 4
Exercise is an important part of a healthy life. If people don't exercise, they will become unhealthy. Nowadays, many people don't get enough exercise ~~due to~~ *because* they have jobs where they sit down all day. Additionally, life is easier. In the old days, people had to wash clothes by hand or make their own bread. ~~Result~~ *As a result*, they were more active in their lives. Also, people didn't have cars in the old days, ~~because~~ *so* they had to walk everywhere. This meant that people were active in their daily life. Now, due to cars and machines which make life easier, people don't do as much. As a result, they become more unfit.

Exercise 5
1 c
2 e
3 d
4 a
5 b

Causes on the lefthand side; *Effects* on the righthand side.

Exercise 6

Model answer

Many health problems today may be caused by modern technology. For example, if children spend too much time playing video games, they may not do enough exercise and may become overweight. Also, people who use computers at work can develop health problems, such as wrist problems or back pain, because they spend all day sitting in the same position. Finally, people spend less time playing healthy sports because they prefer to use social media.

Part 3: Exam practice

Task 2: Model answer

Healthcare is very important for everyone in the world but it can be very expensive. Many people believe that governments should try to prevent illness by making sure everyone in their country has a healthy lifestyle. I agree that preventing illness is better than curing it.

The cost of medical treatment can be high so governments have to think of ways to encourage people to be healthier. If people are healthy, they will not need medical care so often. Many diseases can be prevented if people have good diets, take exercise and give up unhealthy habits such as smoking. If people cannot work or care for themselves or their family due to illness, this will cost governments and taxpayers a lot of money. In my opinion, governments should spend money on producing information leaflets and films which encourage people to follow healthy lifestyles, such as eating plenty of fruit and vegetables, taking regular exercise and giving up smoking. Governments should also try to reduce environmental pollution because this can cause illness and health problems.

However, having a healthy lifestyle cannot prevent all health problems. There are many diseases, such as cancer, which are a result of living in the modern world and which cannot be prevented by a healthy lifestyle. Accidents at work or on the roads will also cause injuries which need medical treatment. If governments focus mainly on prevention, there may be less money for urgent healthcare and many people could suffer.

In conclusion, I believe that governments should provide a balance of prevention and treatment because of the different types of health problem, but their main focus should be on prevention rather than cure.

Unit 12   Transport

Part 1:   Language development

Exercise 1
1 photo b; [rush hour]; traffic jams
2 photo a; commute; crowded
3 photo d; fare; service
4 photo c; abroad; pollution

Exercise 2
2 travelling
3 finding
4 to travel
5 raising
6 to change
7 to see
8 to commute

Exercise 3
2 decided to walk
3 choose / chose to walk
4 appear to feel
5 to resist using

Exercise 4
2 Pollution
3 Public transport
4 Cars
5 a passport
6 the internet

Part 2:   Skills development

Exercise 1
2 S
3 P
4 S
5 P
6 P
7 P
8 S

Exercise 2
1 c
2 b
3 d
4 a

Exercise 3
Suggested answers: (The order of paragraphs here is the correct order for a structure 1 problem and solution essay.)

1 Paragraph B = Introduction: Public transport is essential for going to and from work and school. However it can be expensive and crowded. In my opinion it needs better planning. This essay will describe the problems involved in public transport and suggest possible solutions.

2 Paragraph C = Problem 1 + solutions: Firstly, there is a problem with the cost of public transport. Fares can be very high and so people do not use it and drive cars instead. As a result, the number of cars on the roads increases. In my opinion, fares should be reduced for some people, such as old people and students. Many people also think that driving should be made more expensive. For example, cars could be taxed more and parking could be more expensive. This will make public transport cheaper.

3 Paragraph A = Problem 2 + solutions: Another problem is that sometimes public transport offers poor, slow service. For example, buses and trains stop too frequently which makes journeys slow. Also, there are bad links between buses and trains. Furthermore, there is often a lack of public transport in the countryside. One solution is for buses to have fast lanes on roads and to follow fast routes, without too many stops. Timetables should also be coordinated better. Some people think that country travellers should have cheaper fares.

4 Paragraph D = Conclusion: Although there are many challenges in public transport, there are solutions, and overall I think that public transport which is properly planned is a good thing.

Exercise 4
First of all, air travel is a major ~~causes~~ *cause* of air pollution. The number of flights ~~have~~ *has* increased dramatically over the last thirty years because people travel more for business, holidays and to visit friends and family. The pollution from air travel contributes ~~significant~~ *significantly* to climate change. To reduce the effect of air travel on the environment, governments should spend ~~most~~ *more* money on scientific research. Scientists must try to find a different type of fuel which does not ~~harming~~ *harm* the environment as much. In addition, governments could offer tax ~~reduce~~ *reductions* to airline companies that are more environmentally friendly.

Exercise 5

1 e   cheap
2 a   forms
3 b   to charge
4 f   would
5 c   ~~the~~ (= zero article)
6 d   takes

Part 3: Exam Practice

Task 2: Model answer

Many countries in the world rely on motorways for speedy and efficient transportation, as they are a very convenient way of travelling long distances. However, motorways also have negative aspects such as dangerous traffic, damage to the environment and pollution. In this essay, I will look at some of the problems of motorways and how they can be overcome.

One major problem of motorways is that they can be dangerous. In many countries, the speed limit on motorways is very high. This means that any accidents are more likely to be serious and involve many vehicles. Sometimes in bad weather, several vehicles crash into each other and many people are killed or injured. This problem could be solved in a number of ways. People could have special lessons on how to drive safely on motorways. In addition, special signs could be displayed when driving conditions are bad to make people drive more slowly and safely. Alternatively, the general speed limit could be reduced slightly.

Secondly, motorways can spoil the environment. Motorways often go through beautiful areas and may damage plants and wildlife. This problem could be avoided by building motorways through less beautiful areas or putting some sections in tunnels. In addition, the large amount of traffic on motorways produces both air pollution and noise pollution. However, governments could help to reduce air pollution by making environmentally-friendly cars cheaper. Noise pollution could be reduced by changing motorway surfaces or by putting up sound-proof fences.

Despite the problems of motorways, they are necessary and useful. With careful preparation and planning, the problems they cause could be reduced. People today are also more aware of environmental issues and as a result cars and road transport in general are becoming more environmentally friendly.

Review 4

Exercise 1
1. Some big ~~city~~ *cities* suffer from overcrowding.
2. This is often due *to* people coming to cities for work.
3. London has *grown* rapidly over the last 50 years and now has over 7 million people.
4. This means that moving around the city is difficult in *rush* hour and house prices are very expensive.
5. If I was the mayor of London, I ~~will~~ *would* build more flats on park land, so that more people could afford a place to live.
6. If London will ~~grow~~ *grows* bigger, more public transport will be needed for people who work.
7. The government needs to consider ~~to reduce~~ *reducing* the number of cars coming into cities.
8. People may decide ~~travelling~~ *to travel* by public transport if the system improves.
9. As ~~the~~ *a* result, the roads will be clearer.
10. This would make *transport* in general easier.

Exercise 2
Across 5 – medicine
Across 6 – rush hour
Across 7 – pollute
Down 1 – improve
Down 2 – crowded
Down 3 – factory
Down 4 – junk food

Exercise 3
The information shows the favourite hobbies of 12 to ~~16~~ *14*-year-olds in the 1980s and 2010s and the amount of exercise they have done over this period. The information shows that favourite hobbies have changed, and also that the amount of weekly exercise has decreased for some age groups.

In the 2010s, 12 to 14-year-olds prefer activities which *do not* involve exercise. We can see that in the 1980s just over ~~two thirds~~ *a half* of 12 to 14 year olds named playing sports as their favourite hobby, whereas in the 2010s this number was just under a third. In the 2010s, ~~watching TV~~ *playing computer games* was the most popular hobby.

This change is also reflected in the amount of exercise done by this age group. Although the amount of exercise done by ~~14~~ *12*-year-olds remained about the same throughout this period, the amount of weekly exercise done by 13 and 14-year-olds ~~rose~~ *decreased / went down*. In 1980, 13-year-olds did 13 hours of exercise per week on average. This decreased to 8 hours per week in 2010. This drop was steeper in 14-year-olds, from 11 hours per week in 1980 to ~~3~~ *5* hours per week in 2010.

Exercise 4
1. Pollution in cities needs to be reduced (problem) – make laws to stop car emissions and other pollutants (solution)
Suggested sentence: Pollution in cities could be reduced if the government made more laws to stop car emissions and other pollutants.

2. Overcrowding in cities (effect) – People moving to cities for work (cause)
Suggested sentence: There is overcrowding in cities because a lot of people move to cities to get jobs.

3. Obesity leads to ill health. (problem) – Create free exercise programmes. (solution)
Suggested sentence: Obesity leads to ill health, so free exercise programmes should be created to prevent this.

4. Make driving more expensive. (solution) - Too many cars on the road. (problem)
Suggested sentence: If driving were more expensive, this might reduce the number of cars on the road.

5. Public transport becoming more expensive. (cause) – People using cars more. (effect)
Suggested sentence: Due to the increasing expense of public transport, people are using cars more.

Practice test

Task 1: Model answer

The bar chart shows the number of downloads of four different types of music in millions across five age ranges in 2021 in the USA. The youngest age group is 16–22-yearolds and the oldest is the over 58-year-olds. Different music genres were popular with different age ranges. Overall, young people between the ages of 16 and 31 preferred to download rock and pop music, whereas older people liked jazz and classical music. We can see that rock music was the most popular music genre for three out of five age groups. In all age groups except the 46–57-year-olds and the over 58-year-olds, jazz was downloaded more than classical.

Some age groups preferred to download a specific genre of music. For example, the over 58 group downloaded approximately forty five million classical pieces of music, the 23–31 age group downloaded just over forty million rock recordings in 2010, and the youngest group downloaded almost fifty million pop songs. Downloads of rock music were the highest of all the genres in 2021.

Task 2: Model answer

Happiness is an important part of life. Some people think that we should choose jobs that make us happy. However, others believe that happiness is not important in the workplace and that we should jobs that pay well. I believe that while happiness important, earning good wage is more important.

Firstly, if somebody has a low paying job, they might find life difficult. Everyone needs money in order to fulfil their basic needs such as food and housing. More than this, money helps you do different things and have more experiences in life like travelling and eating out. Having a well-paying job therefore is essential not just for the basics, but for luxuries.

However, people spend a lot of time in their jobs. Normally people work as much as 8 hours a day, and for many demanding jobs people work even more. Therefore, spending this much time doing something they don't enjoy can make their life quite miserable. However, it is important to remember that there are lots of well-paid jobs in the world. By researching a job that is both well paid and that it is enjoyable, people can have the best of both these things.

In conclusion, I believe that being happy is not the most important part of a job and having a good salary can provide more opportunities in life as well as basic things. However, it is possible to be happy at work and earn a lot of money if you find the right job.

Glossary

Key

adj. = adjective
adv. = adverb
conj. = conjunction
n. = noun
phr. = phrase
pl. n. = plural noun
prep. = prep
pron. = pronoun
v. = verb

Unit 1

all **adj. pron. adv.** – used when referring to the whole of something

athletics **pl. n.** – Sporting events such as running, jumping, and throwing are called athletics.

browse **v.** – If you browse the internet, you look for interesting information using a computer.

category **n.** – a set of things with a particular characteristic in common

cricket **n.** – Cricket is an outdoor game played by two teams who take turns at scoring runs by hitting a ball with a bat.

dislike **v.** – If you dislike something or someone, you think they are unpleasant and do not like them.

few **adj. n.** – used to refer to a small number of things

football **n.** – Football is any game in which the ball can be kicked, such as soccer, Australian Rules, rugby union, and American football.

golf **n.** – Golf is a game in which players use special clubs to hit a small ball into holes that are spread out over a large area of grassy land.

guitar **n.** – a musical instrument with six strings which are strummed or plucked

gymnastics **n.** – Gymnastics is physical exercises, especially ones using equipment such as bars and ropes.

heading **n.** – a piece of writing that is written or printed at the top of a page or the column of a table

hockey **n.** – Hockey is a game in which two teams use long sticks with curved ends to try to hit a small ball into the other team's goal.

karate **n.** – Karate is a sport in which people fight each other using only their hands, elbows, feet, and legs.

like **v.** – If you like something or someone, you find them pleasant.

listen to **v.** – to pay attention to a sound

motor racing **n.** – Motor racing is a sport in which fast cars race on a track.

music **n.** – Music is a pattern of sounds performed by people singing or playing instruments.

no **adj.** – none at all or not at all

play **v.** – When you play a sport or match, you take part in it.
    v. – If an actor plays a character in a play or film, he or she performs that role.
    v. – If you play a musical instrument, you produce music from it.
    v. – If you play a CD, you listen to it.

shopping **n.** – When you go shopping, you go to the shops and buy things.

skating **n.** – Skating is an activity in which you slide over a surface, e.g. ice, wearing skates.

social media platform **n.** – a digital application or website used to contact users and form communities online

some **adj. pron.** – You use 'some' to refer to a quantity or number when you are not stating the quantity or number exactly.

sport **n.** – Sports are games and other enjoyable activities which need physical effort and skill.

student **n.** – a person studying at university or college

table **n.** – a set of facts or figures arranged in rows or columns

teenager **n.** – a young person aged 13–19

television **n.** – a piece of electronic equipment which receives pictures and sounds by electrical signals over a distance

tennis **n.** – Tennis is a game played by two or four players on a rectangular court in which a ball is hit by players over a central net.

the internet **n.** – a computer system that allows users to exchange information all over the world

TV **n.** – television

website **n.** – a set of information which is available on the internet

yoga **n.** – Yoga is a type of exercise in which you move your body into various positions in order to become more fit or flexible.

Unit 2

achieve **v.** – If you achieve something, you successfully do it or cause it to happen.

assessment **n.** – a piece of work for a course of study, e.g. an essay, which has to be assessed by a tutor

axis (**pl.** *axes*) **n.** – An axis of a graph is one of the two lines on which the scales of measurement are marked.

bar chart **n.** – a way of showing mathematical information using bars to show quantities

category **n.** – a set of things with a particular characteristic in common

class **n.** – a group of pupils or students taught together, or a lesson that they have together

college **n.** – a place where students study after they have left school

continue **v.** – If you continue to do something, you keep doing it.

course **n.** – a series of lessons or lectures

decide **v.** – If you decide to do something, you choose to do it.

difference **n.** – The difference between two numbers is the amount by which one is less than another.

entrance exam **n.** – an exam students must pass in order to go to a particular school, college or university

essay **n.** – a short piece of writing on a particular subject, for example one done as an exercise by a student

exam **n.** – an official test set to find out your knowledge or skill in a subject

fail **v.** – If you fail an exam, you do not get a satisfactory level or pass.

however **adv.** – You use 'however' when you are adding a comment which contrasts with what has just been said.

humanities **pl. n.** – The humanities are subjects such as literature, philosophy, and history which are concerned with people rather than with science.

language **n.** – the system of words that the people of a country use to communicate with each other

law **n.** – The law is the system of rules developed by the government of a country, which regulate what people may and may not do and deals with people who break these rules.

lecture **n.** – a formal talk intended to teach people about a particular subject *literature* **n.** – Literature consists of novels, plays, and poetry.

local **adj.** – Local means in, near, or belonging to the area in which you live.

mathematics **n.** – Mathematics is the study of numbers, quantities, and shapes.

pass **v.** – If you pass an exam, you achieve a satisfactory level in it.

pass grade **n.** – A pass grade is the grade you must achieve to pass an exam.

rate **n.** – the number of times something happens or the number of examples of it

percentage **n.** – a fraction expressed as a number of hundredths

presentation **n.** – To give a presentation is to give a talk or demonstration to an audience of something you have been studying or working on.

qualification **n.** – something you get when you finish a course of study

quantity **n.** – an amount you can measure or count

range from ... to ... **v.** – to be included in a group of numbers or ages

science **n.** – Science is the study of the nature and behaviour of natural things and the knowledge obtained about them.

social sciences **n.** – subjects which study the way people live in society, e.g. sociology

study **v.** – If you study a particular subject, you spend time learning about it.

subject **n.** – an area of study

teacher **n.** – a person who teaches other people, especially children

university **n.** – a place where students study for degrees

work **n.** – People who have work or who are in work have a job which they are paid to do.

work experience **n.** – a period of time a student spends working temporarily for an employer in order to get experience.

write **v.** – When you write something, you use a pen or pencil to form letters, words, or numbers on a surface.

v. – If you write something such as a poem, a book, or a piece of music, you create it.

Unit 3

activity **n.** – something you do for pleasure

amazing **adj.** – very surprising or remarkable

and **conj.** – You use 'and' to link two or more words or phrases together.

architecture **n.** – the art or practice of designing buildings

art gallery **n.** – a public building where paintings or sculptures are on display

beautiful **adj.** – very attractive or pleasing

because **conj.** – 'Because' is used with a clause that gives the reason for something.

building **n.** – a structure with walls and a roof

but **conj.** – used to introduce an idea that is opposite to what has gone before

concert **n.** – a public performance by musicians

coordination **n.** – the ability to control the movements of the different parts of your body

costume **n.** – a set of clothes worn by an actor

creative **adj.** – Creative activities involve the inventing and developing of original ideas.

cultural **adj.** – relating to the arts generally, or to the arts and customs of a particular society

culture **n.** – Culture refers to the arts and to people's appreciation of them.

n. – The culture of a particular society is its ideas, customs, and art.

dangerous **adj.** – able to or likely to cause hurt or harm

dinosaur **n.** – a large reptile which lived in prehistoric times

drawing **n.** – a picture made with a pencil, pen, or crayon

entrance **n.** – Entrance is the right to enter a place.

exhibition **n.** – a public display of works of art, products, or skills

film **n.** – A film consists of moving pictures that have been recorded so that they can be shown in a cinema or on television.

free **adj.** – If something is free, you can have it without paying for it.

harmless **adj.** – safe to use or be near

interesting **adj.** – making you want to know, learn or hear more

lazy **adj.** – idle and unwilling to work

modern **adj.** – relating to the present time

museum **n.** – a building where many interesting or valuable objects are kept and displayed

musical instrument **n.** – a thing used to make music, e.g. a piano or a guitar

opera **n.** – a play in which the words are sung rather than spoken

painting **n.** – a picture someone has painted

performance **n.** – an entertainment provided for an audience

relax **v.** – If you relax, you become calm and your muscles lose their tension.

sculpture **n.** – a work of art produced by carving or shaping stone or clay

self-motivation **n.** – a feeling of enthusiasm or interest that makes someone want to do something

statement **n.** – something you say or write when you give facts or information in a formal way

terrible **adj.** – very bad or of poor quality

tiring **adj.** – Something that is tiring makes you tired.

traditional **adj.** – Traditional customs or beliefs have existed for a long time without changing.

useful **adj.** – If something is useful, you can use it in order to do something or to help you in some way.

Unit 4

behave **v.** – To behave yourself means to act correctly or properly.

benefit **n.** – If you have the benefit of something, it helps you or improves your life.

can **v.** – If you can do something, it is possible for you to do it or you are allowed to do it.

carer **n.** – someone who looks after a child or another person who cannot look after themselves

childhood **n.** – Someone's childhood is the time when they are a child.

conclusion **n.** – the finish or ending of something

could **v.** – You use 'could' to say that something might happen or might be the case.

daughter **n.** – Someone's daughter is their female child.

economic **adj.** – concerning the management of the money, industry, and trade of a country

family **n.** – a group consisting of parents and their children; also all the people who are related to each other, including aunts and uncles, cousins, and grandparents

father **n.** – A person's father is their male parent.

full-time **adj.** – involving work for the whole of each normal working week

get on with **v.** – If you get on with someone, you like them and are friendly to them.

grandmother **n.** – Your grandmother is your father's mother or your mother's mother.

grandson **n.** – Someone's grandson is the son of their son or daughter.

housework **n.** – work such as cleaning and cooking done in the home

idea **n.** – a plan, suggestion, or thought that you have after thinking about a problem

n. – an opinion or belief

introduction **n.** – a piece of writing at the beginning of an essay, which usually tells you what the essay is about

love **n.** – Love is a strong emotional feeling of affection for someone or something.

might **v.** – If you say something might happen, you mean that it is possible that it will happen.

mother **n.** – Your mother is the woman who gave birth to you.

mother-in-law **n.** – Someone's mother-in-law is the mother of their husband or wife.

only child **n.** – a child who has no brothers or sisters

opinion **n.** – a belief or view

paragraph **n.** – A section of a piece of writing. Paragraphs begin on a new line.

parent **n.** – Your parents are your father and mother.

part-time **adj.** – involving work for only a part of the working day or week

professional **adj.** – Professional means relating to the work of someone who is qualified in a particular profession.

provide **v.** – If you provide something for someone, you give it to them or make it available for them.

role **n.** – Someone's role is their position and function in a situation or society.

rule **n.** – Rules are statements which tell you what you are allowed to do.

save **v.** – to keep money for the future

should **v.** – You use 'should' to give advice or make recommendations.

socialize **v.** – to meet other people socially

society **n.** – Society is the people in a particular country or region.

son **n.** – Someone's son is their male child.

structure **n.** – The structure of something is the way it is made, built, or organized.

support **n.** – Support is help that you give to someone. Financial support is money that is provided for someone or something.

supportive **adj.** – A supportive person is encouraging and helpful to someone who is in difficulty.

traditional **adj.** – Traditional customs or beliefs have existed for a long time without changing.

view **n.** – Your views are your personal opinions.

viewpoint **n.** – Your viewpoint is your attitude towards something.

will **v.** – You use 'will' to indicate that you hope, think, or have evidence that something is going to happen in the future.

Unit 5

accommodation **n.** – a place provided for someone to sleep, live, or work in

amount **n.** – An amount of something is how much there is of it.

aquarium **n.** – a building where fish and other sea creatures are kept in glass tanks filled with water

attraction **n.** – something people visit for interest or pleasure

castle **n.** – a large building with walls or ditches round it to protect it from attack

category **n.** – a set of things with a particular characteristic in common

change **n.** – a difference or alteration in something

city break **n.** – a short holiday in a city

cost **n.** – The cost of something is the amount of money needed to buy it, do it, or make it.

country **n.** – one of the political areas the world is divided into

decrease **v.** – If something decreases or if you decrease it, it becomes less in quantity or size.
  n. – a lessening in the amount of something; also the amount by which something becomes less

drop **v.** – If a level or amount drops, it becomes less.
  n. – a decrease

fall **v.** – If something falls in amount or strength, it becomes less.
  n. – A fall in something is a reduction in its amount or strength.

fast **adv.** – quickly and without delay

festival **n.** – an organized series of events and performances

flight **n.** – A flight is a journey made by flying, usually in an aeroplane.

fluctuate **v.** – If something fluctuates, it changes a lot in an irregular way.

fluctuation **n.** – frequent changes in the amount, level, or number of something

go down **v.** – to decrease

go up **v.** – to increase

gradual **adj.** – happening or changing slowly over a long period of time

gradually **adv.** – happening or changing slowly over a long period of time

hard **adv.** – earnestly or intently

holiday **n.** – a period of time spent away from home for enjoyment

increase **v.** – If something increases, it becomes larger in amount.
  n. – a rise in the number, level, or amount of something

line graph **n.** – a picture that uses lines to show the relationship between numbers or measurements that change

long-haul **adj.** – A long-haul flight is a long journey on an aeroplane.

popularity **n.** – the state of being popular

predict **v.** – If someone predicts an event, they say that it will happen in the future.

price **n.** – The price of something is the amount of money you have to pay to buy it.

quantity **n.** – an amount you can measure or count

rapid **adj.** – happening or moving very quickly

rise **v.** – If an amount rises, it increases.

sharp **adj.** – A sharp change is sudden and significant.

since **prep. conj. adv.** – Since means from a particular time until now.

slightly **adv.** – Slightly means to some degree but not much.

stable **adj.** – not likely to change or come to an end suddenly

steady **adj.** – Something that is steady continues or develops gradually without any interruptions and is unlikely to change suddenly.

tourist **n.** – a person who visits places for pleasure or interest

traveller **n.** – a person who travels

trend **n.** – a change towards doing or being something different

type **n.** – A type of something is a class of it that has common features and belongs to a larger group of related things.

zoo **n.** – a place where live animals are kept so that people can look at them

Unit 6

about **prep. adv.** – approximately and not exactly

actor **n.** – a man or woman whose profession is acting

adult **n.** – a mature and fully developed person or animal

almost **adv.** – very nearly

amount **n.** – An amount of something is how much there is of it.

approximate **adj.** – almost exact

blockbuster **n.** – a film that is very successful

buy **v.** – If you buy something, you obtain it by paying money for it.

cartoon **n.** – a film in which the characters and scenes are drawn

category **n.** – a set of things with a particular characteristic in common

CD **n.** – an abbreviation for 'compact disc'

character **n.** – The characters in a film, play, or book are the people in it.

cinema **n.** – a place where people go to watch films

comedy **n.** – a light-hearted play or film with a happy ending

cost **n.** – The cost of something is the amount of money needed to buy it, do it, or make it.

director **n.** – the person responsible for the making and performance of a programme, play, or film

documentary **n.** – a radio or television programme, or a film, which gives information on real events

DVD **n.** – an abbreviation for 'digital video or digital versatile disc': a type of compact disc that can store large amounts of video and sound information

explorer **n.** – someone who travels to a place that other people do not know much about

explosion **n.** – a sudden violent burst of energy, for example one caused by a bomb

format **n.** – the form that a film, television programme or music recording is produced in

fraction **n.** – In arithmetic, a fraction is a part of a whole number.

genre **n.** – a particular style in literature, art or film

half **n. adj. adv.** – Half refers to one of two equal parts that make up a whole.

movie **n.** – a film

nearly **adv.** – not completely but almost

number **n.** – A number of things is a quantity of them.

per cent **adv.** You use per cent to talk about amounts as a proportion of a hundred. An amount that is 10 per cent (10%) of a larger amount is equal to 10 hundredths of the larger amount.

percentage **n.** – a fraction expressed as a number of hundredths

pie chart **n.** – a circular graph divided into sections to show the relative sizes of things

proportion **n.** – A proportion of an amount or group is a part of it.

n. – The proportion of one amount to another is its size in comparison with the other amount.

publicity **n.** – Information or actions that aim to attract the public's attention to someone or something.

quantity **n.** – an amount you can measure or count

quarter **n.** – one of four equal parts

reason **n.** – The reason for something is the fact or situation which explains why it happens or which causes it to happen.

romantic **adj.** – A romantic play, film, or story describes or represents a love affair.

sale **n.** – The sales of a product are the numbers that are sold.

section **n.** – A section of something is one of the parts it is divided into.

sell **v.** – If you sell something, you let someone have it in return for money.

share **n.** – A share of something is a portion of it.

soundtrack **n.** – The soundtrack of a film is the part you hear.

spaceship **n.** – a spacecraft that carries people through space

special effects **n.** – unusual images or sounds that are created artificially for a film

story **n.** – a description of imaginary people and events written or told to entertain people

n. – The story of something or someone is an account of the important events that have happened to them.

television **n.** – a piece of electronic equipment which receives pictures and sounds by electrical signals over a distance

the internet **n.** – a computer system that allows users to exchange information all over the world

third **n.** – one of three equal parts

three quarters **n.** – three of four equal parts of something

thriller **n.** – a book, film, or play that tells an exciting story about dangerous or mysterious events

video **n.** – a sound and picture recording which can be played back on a television set

visitor **n.** – someone who visits a place or a person

watch **v.** – If you watch something, you look at it for some time and pay close attention to what is happening.

winner **n.** – The winner of a prize, race, or competition is the person or thing that wins it.

worldwide **adj.** – throughout the world

Unit 7

accident **n.** – an unexpected event in which people are injured or killed

account **n.** – an arrangement with a company or internet provider to use a service they provide

activity **n.** – something you do for pleasure

addictive **adj.** – If a drug is addictive, the people who take it cannot stop.

advantage **n.** – An advantage is a way in which one thing is better than another.

afford **v.** – If you can afford to do something, you have enough money or time to do it.

also **adv.** – in addition to something that has just been mentioned

although conj. – in spite of the fact that

argument **n.** – a point or a set of reasons you use to try to convince people about something

arrangements **n.** – practical plans for managing the details of a meeting or event

ban **v.** – If something is banned, or if you are banned from doing it or using it, you are not allowed to do it or use it.

boss **n.** – Someone's boss is the person in charge of the place where they work.

break **v.** – If important news breaks, it becomes known to the public.

call **v.** – If you call someone, you telephone them.

camera **n.** – a piece of equipment used for taking photographs or for filming

charge **n.** – the price that you have to pay for something

chat **v.** – When people chat, they talk to each other in a friendly way.

check **v.** – If you check something, or if you make a check on it, you make sure that it is satisfactory, safe, or correct.

communicate **v.** – If you communicate with someone, you keep in touch with them.

communication **n.** – Communication is the process by which people or animals exchange information.

company **n.** – a business that sells goods or provides a service *computer* **n.** – an electronic machine that can quickly make calculations or store and find information

contact **n.** – If you are in contact with someone, you regularly talk to them or write to them.

cross **v.** – to go to the other side of a road

dangerous **adj.** – able to or likely to cause hurt or harm

delayed **adj.** – late

disadvantage **n.** – an unfavourable or harmful circumstance

distract **v.** – If something distracts you, your attention is taken away from what you are doing.

download **v.** – If you download data you transfer it from the memory of one computer to that of another, especially over the internet.

effect **n.** – a direct result of someone or something on another person or thing

efficient **adj.** – Something or someone that is efficient does a job successfully, without wasting time or energy.

emergency **n.** – an unexpected and serious event which needs immediate action to deal with it

expensive **adj.** – costing a lot of money

fix **v.** – to mend something

focus on **v.** – to concentrate on something

friendly **adj.** – If you are friendly to someone, you behave in a kind and pleasant way to them.

furthermore **adv.** – Furthermore is used to introduce a statement adding to or supporting the previous one.

go wrong **v.** – If a machine or piece of equipment goes wrong, it stops working correctly.

gossip **n.** – Gossip is informal conversation, often concerning people's private affairs.

idea **n.** – a plan, suggestion, or thought that you have after thinking about a problem
    n. – an opinion or belief

identity **n.** – the characteristics that make you who you are

illegal **adj.** – If something is illegal, the law says that it is not allowed.

industry **n.** – Industry is the work and processes involved in manufacturing things in factories.

job **n.** – the work that someone does to earn money

lose **v.** – If you lose something, you cannot find it, or you no longer have it because it has been taken away from you.

main **adj.** – most important

mobile phone **n.** – a small portable telephone

moreover **adv.** – You use moreover to introduce a piece of information that adds to or supports the previous statement.

music **n.** – Music is a pattern of sounds performed by people singing or playing instruments.

musician **n.** – a person who plays a musical instrument as their job or hobby

negative **adj.** – unpleasant, depressing, or harmful

news **n.** – News is information about things that have happened.

online **adj.** – Online means available on or connected to the internet.

pay **v.** – to give money in order to buy something

pedestrian **n.** – someone who is walking

point **n.** – a quality

productivity **n.** – Productivity is the rate at which things are produced or dealt with.

question **n.** – a problem that needs to be discussed

relative **n.** – Your relatives are the members of your family.

replace **v.** – When one thing replaces another, the first thing takes the place of the second.

steal **v.** – To steal something means to take it without permission and without intending to return it.

stranger **n.** – someone you have never met before

streaming **v.** – a way of moving data from the internet directly to a user's computer or phone screen without needing to download it.

technology **n.** – Technology is the application of science and scientific knowledge for practical purposes in industry, farming, medicine, or business.

text **v.** – If you text someone, you send them a text message.

true **adj.** – A true story or statement is based on facts and is not made up.

up-to-date **adj.** – being the newest thing of its kind
 adj. – having the latest information

waste of time **n.** – something you spend time doing which does not have a useful result

website **n.** – a set of information which is available on the internet

workplace **n.** – Your workplace is the building or company where you work.

yet **conj.** – You can use 'yet' to introduce a fact which is rather surprising.

Unit 8

accommodation **n.** – a place provided for someone to sleep, live, or work in

according to **prep.** – in the opinion of

action **n.** – something that is done

although **conj.** – in spite of the fact that

approach **n.** – An approach to a situation or problem is a way of thinking about it or dealing with it.

argue **v.** – If you argue that something is the case, you give reasons why you think it is so.

argument **n.** – a point or a set of reasons you use to try to convince people about something

aspect **n.** – An aspect of something is one of its features.

attitude **n.** – Your attitude to someone or something is the way you think about them and behave towards them.

believe **v.** – If you believe that something is true, you accept that it is true.

business **n.** – Business is work relating to the buying and selling of goods and services.

change **n.** – a difference or alteration in something

citizen **n.** – The citizens of a country or city are the people who live in it or belong to it.

claim **v.** – If you claim that something is the case, you say that it is the case.

clothing **n.** – the clothes people wear

counsellor **n.** – someone whose job is to give advice to people

culture **n.** – The culture of a particular society is its ideas, customs, and art.

economy **n.** – The economy of a country is the system it uses to organize and manage its money, industry, and trade; also used of the wealth that a country gets from business and industry.

education **n.** – the process of gaining knowledge and understanding through learning or the system of teaching people

effect **n.** – a direct result of someone or something on another person or thing

employee **n.** – a person who is paid to work for another person or for an organization

employer **n.** – Someone's employer is the person or organization that they work for.

enjoy **v.** – If you enjoy something, you find pleasure and satisfaction in it.

expensive **adj.** – costing a lot of money

experience **n.** – Experience consists of all the things that you have done or that have happened to you.

factor **n.** – something that helps to cause a result

family **n.** – a group consisting of parents and their children; also all the people who are related to each other, including aunts and uncles, cousins, and grandparents

famous **adj.** – very well-known

financial **adj.** – relating to or involving money

friend **n.** – Your friends are people you know well and like to spend time with.

future **n.** – The future is the period of time after the present.

government **n.** – The government is the group of people who govern a country.

happiness **n.** – a feeling of great contentment or pleasure

happy **adj.** – feeling, showing, or producing contentment or pleasure

health **n.** – Health is the state of being free from disease and feeling well.

hobby **n.** – something that you do for enjoyment in your spare time

important **adj.** – Something that is important is very significant, valuable, or necessary.

improve **v.** – If something improves or if you improve it, it gets better or becomes more valuable.

in my opinion **phr.** – used for introducing the opinion of the speaker or writer

in addition **phr.** – used for adding an extra piece of information to what has been said or written

income **n.** – the money a person earns

inherit **v.** – If you inherit money or property, you receive it from someone who has died.

investment **n.** – An investment is an amount of money that you invest, or the thing that you invest it in.

job **n.** – the work that someone does to earn money

living standard **n.** – the type of life that a person has depending on the amount of money they have

lower **v.** – To lower something also means to make it less in value or amount.

manage **v.** – If you manage time, money, or other resources, you deal with them carefully and do not waste them.

money **n.** – Money is the coins or banknotes that you use to buy something.

move **v.** – If you move, or move house, you go to live in a different house.

negative **adj.** – A fact, situation, or experience that is negative is unpleasant, depressing, or harmful.

on the other hand **phr.** – used to introduce an opposite point of view

opinion **n.** – a belief or view

own **v.** – If you own something, it belongs to you.

personal **adj.** – Personal means belonging or relating to a particular person rather than to people in general.

pet **n.** – a tame animal kept at home

positive **adj.** – If you are positive, you are hopeful and confident, and think of the good aspects of a situation rather than the bad ones.

possessions **n.** – the things that you own

poverty **n.** – the state of being very poor

price **n.** – The price of something is the amount of money you have to pay to buy it.

problem **n.** – an unsatisfactory situation that causes difficulties

raise **v.** – If you raise the rate or level of something, you increase it.

reason **n.** – If you have reason to believe or feel something, there are definite reasons why you believe it or feel it.

receive **v.** – When you receive something, someone gives it to you, or you get it after it has been sent to you.

reduce **v.** – To reduce something means to make it smaller in size or amount.

religion **n.** – a system of religious belief

rent **v.** – If you rent something, you pay the owner a regular sum of money in return for being able to use it.

n. – Rent is the amount of money you pay regularly to rent land or accommodation.

rich **adj.** – Someone who is rich has a lot of money and possessions.

salary **n.** – a regular monthly payment to an employee

save **v.** – to keep money for the future

savings **n.** – the money that you have saved, especially in a bank or a building society

say **v.** – to give an opinion

serious **adj.** – A serious problem or situation is very bad and worrying.

similarly **adv.** – used to say that there is a correspondence or similarity between the way two things happen or are done.

solve **v.** – If you solve a problem or a question, you find a solution or answer to it.

spend **v.** – to use money to pay for things

v. – to use time for some activity

state **v.** – If you state something, you say it or write it, especially in a formal way.

status **n.** – A person's status is their position and importance in society.

stress **n.** – Stress is worry and nervous tension.

stressed **adj.** – feeling tension or anxiety because of the problems in your life

stressful **adj.** – causing someone to feel stress

success **n.** – Success is the achievement of something you have been trying to do.

suggest **v.** – If you suggest a plan or idea to someone, you mention it as a possibility for them to consider.

tax **n.** – Tax is an amount of money that the people in a country have to pay to the government so that it can provide public services such as health care and education.

v. – If a sum of money is taxed, a certain amount of it has to be paid to the government.

think **v.** – If you think something, you have the opinion that it is true or the case.

traditional **adj.** – Traditional customs or beliefs have existed for a long time without changing.

wealth **n.** – Wealth is the large amount of money or property which someone owns.

wealthy **adj.** – having a large amount of money, property, or other valuable things

work **v.** – People who work have a job which they are paid to do.

n. – People who have work or who are in work have a job which they are paid to do.

worry **n.** – Worry is a feeling of unhappiness and unease caused by a problem or by thinking of something unpleasant that might happen.

yet conj. – You can use 'yet' to introduce a fact which is rather surprising.

Unit 9

absorb **v.** – If something absorbs liquid or gas, it soaks it up.

acid rain **n.** – rain polluted by acid in the atmosphere which has come from factories

after conj. – If something happens or is done after a particular event or date, it happens or is done during the period of time that follows it.

after conj. – used to introduce a clause which describes something done in the period of time following something else

atmosphere **n.** – the air and other gases that surround a planet; also the air in a particular place

bale **n.** – a large bundle of something, such as paper or hay, tied tightly *barn* **n.** – a large farm building used for storing crops or animal food

building **n.** – a structure with walls and a roof

camel **n.** – A large mammal with either one or two humps on its back. Camels live in hot desert areas and are sometimes used for carrying things.

carry **v.** – To carry something is to hold it and take it somewhere.

chemical **n.** – Chemicals are substances manufactured by chemistry.

climate **n.** – The climate of a place is the typical weather conditions there.

cloud **n.** – a mass of water vapour, smoke, or dust that forms in the air and is seen floating in the sky

combine harvester **n.** – a large machine used on a farm for cutting grain crops, and removing and cleaning the seeds

cow **n.** – a large animal kept on farms for its milk

crater **n.** – the hole at the top of a volcano

crop **n.** – a plant grown for food

cut **v.** – If you cut something, you use a knife, scissors, or some other sharp tool to mark it or remove parts of it.

damage **v.** – To damage something means to harm or spoil it.

deposit **v.** – If you deposit something, you put it down or leave it somewhere.

destroy **v.** – To destroy something means to damage it so much that it is completely ruined.

diagram **n.** – a drawing that shows or explains something

die **v.** – When people, animals, or plants die, they stop living.

disaster **n.** – an event or accident that causes great distress or destruction

Earth **n.** – the planet we live on

elephant **n.** – a very large four-legged mammal with a long trunk, large ears, and ivory tusks

erupt **v.** – When a volcano erupts, it violently throws out a lot of hot lava and ash.

factory **n.** – a building or group of buildings where goods are made in large quantities

fall **v.** – If someone or something falls or falls over, they drop towards the ground.

farmer **n.** – a person who owns or manages a farm

feed **v.** – To feed a person or animal is to give them food.

field **n.** – an enclosed area of land where crops are grown or animals are kept

finally **adv.** – You use 'finally' to introduce a final point or topic.

first **adv.** – You use 'first' to introduce the first of a number of things that you want to say.

first of all **adv.** – You use 'first' or 'first of all' to introduce the first of a number of things that you want to say.

firstly **adv.** – You use 'firstly' to mention the first in a series of items.

flow **v.** – to move steadily and continuously

flower **n.** – the brightly-coloured part of a plant at the end of the stem
   v. – when a plant's flowers appear and open

forest **n.** – a large area of trees growing close together

form **v.** – When someone forms something or when it forms, it is created, organized, or started.

gas **n.** – any airlike substance that is not liquid or solid, such as oxygen or the gas used as a fuel in heating

gazelle **n.** – a small antelope found in Africa and Asia

glacier **n.** – a huge frozen river of slow-moving ice

grass **n.** – Grass is the common green plant that grows on lawns and in parks.

greenhouse effect **n.** – the gradual rise in temperature in the earth's atmosphere due to heat being absorbed from the sun and being trapped by gases such as carbon dioxide in the air around the earth

grow **v.** – If a tree or plant grows somewhere, it is alive there.

v. – When people grow plants, they plant them and look after them.

harvest **v.** – To harvest food means to gather it when it is ripe.

heat **n.** – Heat is warmth or the quality of being hot; also the temperature of something that is warm or hot.

high **adj.** – tall or a long way above the ground

hunt **v.** – To hunt means to chase wild animals to kill them for food or for sport.

ice **n.** – water that has frozen solid

inhabit **v.** – If you inhabit a place, you live there.

insect **n.** – a small creature with six legs, and usually wings

irrigation **n.** – supplying land with water in order to grow crops

kill **v.** – To kill a person, animal, or plant is to make them die.

lava **n.** – Lava is the very hot liquid rock that comes shooting out of an erupting volcano, and becomes solid as it cools.

law **n.** – one of the rules established by a government or a religion, which tells people what they may or may not do

liquid **n.** – any substance which is not a solid or a gas, and which can be poured

low **adj.** – Something that is low is close to the ground, or measures a short distance from the ground to the top.

machine **n.** – a piece of equipment which uses electricity or power from an engine to make it work

magma **n.** – Magma is a hot liquid within the earth's crust which forms igneous rock when it solidifies.

melt **v.** – When something melts or when you melt it, it changes from a solid to a liquid because it has been heated.

mountain **n.** – a very high piece of land with steep sides

movement **n.** – Movement involves changing position or going from one place to another.

natural **adj.** – existing or happening in nature

next **adv.** – coming immediately after something else

physical **adj.** – relating to real things that can be touched or seen

pick **v.** – If you pick a flower or fruit, or pick something from a place, you remove it with your fingers.

pick up **v.** – to lift up from a surface

plant **n.** – a living thing that grows in the earth and has stems, leaves, and roots

polluted **adj.** – dirty or dangerous because of chemicals or sewage

pollution **n.** – Pollution of the environment happens when dirty or dangerous substances get into the air, water, or soil.

process **n.** – a series of actions intended to achieve a particular result or change

produce **v.** – To produce something is to make it or cause it.

product **n.** – something that is made to be sold

protect **v.** – To protect someone or something is to prevent them from being harmed or damaged.

v. – to prevent a particular animal, plant, or area of land from being harmed or damaged by making it illegal to do so

radiation **n.** – the stream of particles given out by a radioactive substance

rainforest **n.** – a dense forest of tall trees in a tropical area where there is a lot of rain *reflect* **v.** – When light or heat is reflected off a surface, it is sent back from the surface rather than passing through it.

reservoir **n.** – a lake used for storing water before it is supplied to people

rise **v.** – If something rises, it moves upwards.

rock **n.** – a large piece of rock

scatter **v.** – To scatter things means to throw or drop them all over an area.

scientist **n.** – an expert in one of the sciences who does work connected with it

secondly **adv.** – You say 'secondly' when you want to make a second point or give a second reason for something.

seed **n.** – The seeds of a plant are the small, hard parts from which new plants can grow.

separate **v.** – To separate people or things means to cause them to be apart from each other.

snow **n.** – Snow consists of flakes of ice crystals which fall from the sky in cold weather.

store **v.** – When you store something somewhere, you keep it there until it is needed.

storm **n.** – When there is a storm, there is heavy rain, a strong wind, and often thunder and lightning.

straw **n.** – Straw is the dry, yellowish stalks from cereal crops.

sun **n.** – The sun is the star providing heat and light for the planets revolving around it in our solar system.

surface **n.** – The surface of something is the top or outside area of it.

system **n.** – an organized way of doing or arranging something according to a fixed plan or set of rules

temperature **n.** – The temperature of something is how hot or cold it is.

then **adv.** – at a particular time in the past or future
  adv. – in that case

tiger **n.** – a large meat-eating animal of the cat family. It comes from Asia and has an orange coloured coat with black stripes

transport **v.** – When goods or people are transported from one place to another, they are moved there.

vent **n.** – a hole in something through which gases and smoke can escape and fresh air can enter

volcano **n.** – a hill with an opening through which lava, gas, and ash burst out from inside the earth onto the surface

warm **adj.** – Something that is warm has some heat, but not enough to be hot.
  v. – If you warm something, you heat it up gently so that it stops being cold.

water **v.** – If you water a plant or an animal, you give it water to drink.

wheat **n.** – Wheat is a cereal plant grown for its grain which is used to make flour.

when **conj.** – You use 'when' to introduce a clause where you refer to the time at which something happens.

wildlife **n.** – Wildlife means wild animals and plants.

world **n.** – The world is the earth, the planet we live on.

Unit 10

accommodation **n.** – a place provided for someone to sleep, live, or work in

alone **adj. adv.** – not with other people or things

alter **v.** – If something alters or if you alter it, it changes.

apartment **n.** – a set of rooms for living in, usually on one floor of a building

area **n.** – a particular part of a place, country, or the world
  n. – The area of a piece of ground or a surface is the amount of space it covers, measured in square metres or square feet.

availability **n.** – the state of being able to be obtained or used

available **adj.** – Something that is available can be obtained.

average **adj.** – Average means standard or normal.

business **n.** – Business is work relating to the buying and selling of goods and services.

business park **n.** – a special area of land used for offices and small factories

clothing **n.** – the clothes people wear

convert **v.** – To convert one thing into another is to change it so that it becomes the other thing.

cost **n.** – The cost of something is the amount of money needed to buy it, do it, or make it.

decrease **v.** – If something decreases or if you decrease it, it becomes less in quantity or size.
  n. – a lessening in the amount of something; also the amount by which something becomes less

detail **n.** – Detail is all the small features that make up the whole of something.

electricity **n.** – Electricity is a form of energy used for heating and lighting, and to provide power for machines.

entertainment **n.** – anything people watch or do for pleasure

expand **v.** – If something expands or you expand it, it becomes larger in number or size.

expenses **n.** – money that you spend while doing your job and which your employer later gives back to you

factory **n.** – a building or group of buildings where goods are made in large quantities

fast food **n.** – hot food that is prepared and served quickly after you have ordered it

flat **n.** – In British English, a flat is a set of rooms for living in, that is part of a larger building.

gas **n.** – any air-like substance that is not liquid or solid, such as oxygen or the gas used as a fuel in heating

grow **v.** – To grow means to increase in size or amount.

high **adj.** – great in degree, quantity, or intensity

housing **n.** – Housing is the buildings in which people live.

improve **v.** – If something improves or if you improve it, it gets better or becomes more valuable.

income **n.** – the money a person earns

increase **v.** – If something increases, it becomes larger in amount.
  n. – a rise in the number, level, or amount of something

industrial **adj.** – relating to industry

industrial area **n.** – a special area of land used for factories

land **n.** – Land is an area of ground.

landscape **n.** – The landscape is the view over an area of open land.

low **adj.** – Low means small in value or amount.

monthly **adj.** – Monthly describes something that happens or appears once a month.

office **n.** – a room or a part of a building where people work sitting at desks

park **n.** – a public area with grass and trees

population **n.** – The people who live in a place, or the number of people living there.

price **n.** – The price of something is the amount of money you have to pay to buy it.

property **n.** – land and the buildings on it

purpose **n.** – The purpose of something is the reason for it.

reduce **v.** – To reduce something means to make it smaller in size or amount.

regulation **n.** – Regulations are official rules.

rent **v.** – If you rent something, you pay the owner a regular sum of money in return for being able to use it.

residential **adj.** – used for houses rather than for offices or shops

rise **n.** – an increase

salary **n.** – a regular monthly payment to an employee

shop **n.** – a place where things are sold

shopping centre **n.** – a group of shops, banks and businesses all built next to each other

spend **v.** – When you spend money, you buy things with it.

stable **adj.** – not likely to change or come to an end suddenly

traffic **n.** – all the vehicles moving along the roads in an area

transform **v.** – If something is transformed, it is changed completely.

use **n.** – when something is used for a particular purpose

Unit 11

absence **n.** – a period of time when someone is not at work or school

activity **n.** – something you do for pleasure

afford **v.** – If you can afford to do something, you have enough money or time to do it.

availability **n.** – the state of being able to be obtained or used

cancer **n.** – a serious disease in which abnormal cells in a part of the body increase rapidly, causing growths

cause **n.** – The cause of something is the thing that makes it happen.

common cold **n.** – an infection which gives you a sore throat and makes you sneeze a lot, caused by a virus

condition **n.** – a requirement that must be met for something else to be possible

cosmetic surgery **n.** – surgery that is done to improve the appearance of a part of the body

cure **v.** – To cure an illness is to end it.
    n. – A cure for an illness is something that cures it.

die **v.** – When people, animals, or plants die, they stop living.

diet **n.** – Someone's diet is the usual food that they eat.

disease **n.** – an unhealthy condition in people, animals, or plants

doctor **n.** – a person who is qualified in medicine and treats people who are ill

effect **n.** – a direct result of someone or something on another person or thing

essential **adj.** – vitally important and absolutely necessary

exercise **n.** – Exercise is any activity which you do to get fit or remain healthy.

face-to-face **adj.** – Face-to-face activities are ones In which you meet and talk to someone directly.

fat **adj.** – Someone who is fat has too much weight on their body.

fit **adj.** – healthy and physically strong

free **adj.** – If something is free, you can have it without paying for it.

harmless **adj.** – safe to use or be near

health **n.** – Your health is the condition of your body.
    n. – Health is also the state of being free from disease and feeling well.

healthcare **n.** – the services that look after people's health

healthy **adj.** – Someone who is healthy is fit and strong and does not have any diseases.
    adj. – Something that is healthy is good for you.

hospital **n.** – a place where sick and injured people are treated and cared for

if conj. – on the condition that

ill **adj.** – unhealthy or sick

illness **n.** – Illness is the experience of being ill.
n. – a particular disease

junk food **n.** – Junk food is food low in nutritional value which is eaten as well as or instead of proper meals.

lack **n.** – If there is a lack of something, it is not present when or where it is needed.

lifestyle **n.** – the way you live, the things you normally do

live **v.** – To live means to be alive.

luxury **n.** – something that you enjoy very much but do not have very often, usually because it is expensive

medicine **n.** – a substance that you drink or swallow to help cure an illness

minor **adj.** – not as important or serious as other things

negative **adj.** – A fact, situation, or experience that is negative is unpleasant, depressing, or harmful.

obesity **n.** – when someone is extremely fat

overweight **adj.** – too fat, and therefore unhealthy

patient **n.** – a person receiving medical treatment from a doctor or in a hospital

pay **v.** – When you pay money to someone, you give it to them because you are buying something or owe it to them.

population **n.** – The population of a place is the people who live there, or the number of people living there.

positive **adj.** – hopeful and confident, and thinking of the good aspects of a situation rather than the bad ones.

prevent **v.** – If you prevent something, you stop it from happening or being done.

problem **n.** – an unsatisfactory situation that causes difficulties

ready meal **n.** – a pre-prepared meal sold in a shop that is ready to eat when heated up

result **n.** – The result of an action or situation is the situation that is caused by it.

smoke **v.** – When someone smokes a cigarette or pipe, they suck smoke from it into their mouth and blow it out again.

social media **n.** – Internet websites which allow people to keep in touch with friends and family.

suffer **v.** – If someone is suffering pain, or suffering as a result of an unpleasant situation, they are badly affected by it.

tax **n.** – Tax is an amount of money that the people in a country have to pay to the government so that it can provide public services such as healthcare and education.
v. – If a sum of money is taxed, a certain amount of it has to be paid to the government.

training **n.** – the process of teaching someone how to do a particular job

treat **v.** – When a doctor treats a patient or an illness, he or she gives them medical care and attention.

unfit **adj.** – in unhealthy or poor condition

unhealthy **adj.** – likely to cause illness
adj. – An unhealthy person is often ill.

Unit 12

abroad **adv.** – in a foreign country

accident **n.** – an unexpected event in which people are injured or killed

accommodation **n.** – a place provided for someone to sleep, live, or work in

airport **n.** – a place where people go to catch planes

alternative **adj.** – describing something that exists or that you can do instead of something else

appear **v.** – If something appears to be a certain way, it seems or looks that way.

busy **adj.** – A busy place is full of people doing things or moving about.

car **n.** – a four-wheeled road vehicle with room for a small number of people

catch **v.** – If you catch a bus or train, you get on it and travel somewhere.

challenge **n.** – something that is new and exciting but requires a lot of effort

change **v.** – When something changes or when you change it, it becomes different.

choose **v.** – To choose something is to decide to have it or do it.

city **n.** – a large town where many people live and work

commute **v.** – People who commute travel a long distance to work every day.

consider **v.** – To consider something is to think about it carefully.

coordinate **v.** – To coordinate an activity is to organize the people or things involved in it.

crowded **adj.** – A crowded place is full of people.

decide **v.** – If you decide to do something, you choose to do it.

distance **n.** – The distance between two points is how far it is between them.

drive **v.** – To drive a vehicle means to operate it and control its movements.

driving test **n.** – an exam drivers must pass before they are allowed to drive on the roads

effect **n.** – a direct result of someone or something on another person or thing

enjoy **v.** – If you enjoy something, you find pleasure and satisfaction in it.

environment **n.** – The environment is the natural world around us.

environmentally friendly **adj.** – describes something which does not damage the environment

expect **v.** – If you expect something to happen, you believe that it will happen.

v. – If you are expecting somebody or something, you believe that they are going to arrive or to happen.

expensive **adj.** – costing a lot of money

fare **n.** – the amount charged for a journey on a bus, train, or plane

fast lane **n.** – the lane of a motorway where drivers can overtake other vehicles

flight **n.** – a journey made by flying, usually in an aeroplane

fuel **n.** – Fuel is a substance such as coal or petrol that is burned to provide heat or power.

harm **v.** – To harm someone or something means to injure or damage them.

healthy **adj.** – Someone who is healthy is fit and strong and does not have any diseases.

adj. – Something that is healthy is good for you.

level **n.** – a point on a scale which measures the amount, importance, or difficulty of something

limit **v.** – To limit something means to prevent it from becoming bigger, spreading, or making progress.

lorry **n.** – a large vehicle for transporting goods by road

motorway **n.** – a wide road built for fast travel over long distances

noise pollution **n.** – noise that is annoying or harmful to people in the place where they live or work and that they have no control over

passenger **n.** – a person travelling in a vehicle, aircraft, or ship

passport **n.** – an official identification document which you need to show when you travel abroad

plan **v.** – If you are planning to do something, you intend to do it.

plane **n.** – a vehicle with wings and engines that enable it to fly *policy* **n.** – a set of plans, especially in politics or business

pollute **v.** – To pollute water or air is to make it dirty and dangerous to use or live in.

pollution **n.** – Pollution of the environment happens when dirty or dangerous substances get into the air, water, or soil.

price **n.** – The price of something is the amount of money you have to pay to buy it.

problem **n.** – an unsatisfactory situation that causes difficulties

promise **v.** – If you promise to do something, you say that you will definitely do it.

public transport **n.** – buses, trains, etc. that everyone can use

reduce **v.** – To reduce something means to make it smaller in size or amount.

resist **v.** – If you resist something, you refuse to accept it and try to prevent it.

road tax **n.** – a tax paid by vehicle drivers for using the roads

rush hour **n.** – The rush hour is one of the busy parts of the day when most people are travelling to or from work.

service **n.** – The level or standard of service provided by an organization or company is the amount or quality of the work it can do for you.

significant **adj.** – A significant amount of something is large enough to be important or noticeable.

solution **n.** – a way of dealing with a problem or difficult situation

source **n.** – The source of something is the person, place, or thing that it comes from.

stress **n.** – Stress is worry and nervous tension.

stressed **adj.** – feeling tension or anxiety because of the problems in your life

suggest **v.** – If you suggest a plan or idea to someone, you mention it as a possibility for them to consider.

tax **n.** – Tax is an amount of money that the people in a country have to pay to the government so that it can provide public services such as healthcare and education

v. – If a sum of money is taxed, a certain amount of it has to be paid to the government.

timetable **n.** – a list of the times when particular trains, boats, buses, or aeroplanes arrive and depart

traffic **n.** – Traffic refers to all the vehicles that are moving along the roads in an area.

traffic jam **n.** – a line of vehicles waiting behind something that is blocking the road

train **n.** – a number of carriages or trucks which are pulled by a railway engine

transport **n.** – Vehicles that you travel in are referred to as transport.

travel **v.** – To travel is to go from one place to another.
n. – Travel is the act of travelling.

underground **n.** – The underground is a railway system in which trains travel in tunnels below ground.

vehicle **n.** – a machine, often with an engine, used for transporting people or goods

walk **v.** – When you walk, you move along by putting one foot in front of the other on the ground.

want **v.** – If you want something, you feel a desire to have it.